CULTIVATING
the Missional Church

CULTIVATING
the Missional Church
New Soil for Growing Vestries and Leaders

RANDOLPH C. FEREBEE

Morehouse Publishing
NEW YORK · HARRISBURG · DENVER

Unless otherwise noted, the Scripture quotations contained herein are from the New Revised Standard Version Bible, copyright © 1989 by the Division of Christian Education of the National Council of Churches of Christ in the U.S.A. Used by permission. All rights reserved.

Every effort has been made to trace the copyright owners of material included in this book. The author and publishers would be grateful if any omissions or inaccuracies could be brought to their attention for correction in any future edition.

The Traditional Approach and the Appreciative Approach graphics on pp. 96 and 97 are © Dave Potter. Used by permission.

The study guide on p. 23 in the downloadable section was created by Steve Conway and © Reggie McNeal. Used by permission.

Morehouse Publishing, 4775 Linglestown Road, Harrisburg, PA 17112
Morehouse Publishing, 445 Fifth Avenue, New York, NY 10016
Morehouse Publishing is an imprint of Church Publishing Incorporated.

www.churchpublishing.org

Cover design by Laurie Klein Westhafer

Typeset by Beth Oberholtzer Design

Library of Congress Cataloging-in-Publication Data

Ferebee, Randolph C.
    Cultivating the missional church : new soil for growing vestries and leaders / Randolph C. Ferebee.
        p.   cm.
    Includes bibliographical references.
    ISBN 978-0-8192-2823-9 (pbk.) -- ISBN 978-0-8192-2824-6 (ebook) 1. Church renewal. 2. Christianity--21st century. 3. Mission of the church. 4. Postmodernism--Religious aspects--Christianity. 5. Missional church movement 6. Emerging church movement. 7. Episcopal Church. I. Title.
BV600.3.F47   2012
253--dc23

2012028905

Printed in the United States of America

for Jonathan, Matthew, Sally,
Allyson, Grayson, Hutch,
George, Park, and Judy

Contents

Preface ix
Appreciation xi
Introduction 1
Prologue: Setting the Context 5

PART ONE

Chapter 1: *A Reordered Path of* GOVERNANCE 17
Chapter 2: *Cultivating Health through* MODELING 22
Chapter 3: *New Roots through* COLLABORATION 27
Chapter 4: *Cultivating Leaders as* CHAMPIONS 30
Chapter 5: *Raising Up and Tapping the* CATALYSTS 33
Chapter 6: *The Way Forward in* MISSION 36
Chapter 7: *Principled Practices by Keeping* COVENANT 43
Chapter 8: *Staying Grounded as* DISCIPLES 47
Chapter 9: *Growth Is Grounded in Positive* CHANGE 50
Chapter 10: *Vestry as a Seedbed for* LEADERSHIP 55
Epilogue 63
Works Consulted 69

PART TWO
Resources

A. Movements and Shifts in the Church of Today 75
B. Vestry Meetings 81
C. The Principle of Subsidiarity 91
D. Appreciative Inquiry Primer 93
E. Introduction to Asset-Based Ministry 98

F. The Five Marks of Mission 104

G. The Story We Tell and the Story God Tells 107

H. A Primer on Permission-Giving Churches 112

I. Creating a Vestry Covenant ➤ 115

J. Bible Study ➤ 117

K. Using an Action-Reflection Model ➤ 122

L. Navigating Church Conflict 125

M. Competencies Self-Assessment ➤ 129

N. Introduction to Servant Leadership 130

Downloadable only:

O. Network Theory and Churches ➤

P. Congregational Life Cycle ➤

Q. Discussion Guide: *Missional Renaissance* ➤

➤ *Downloadable resources available from*
www.churchpublishing.org/cultivatingthemissionalchurch

Preface

You are reading this book because you are a leader. You may be an *intentional* leader. Usually intentional leaders are those who have received ordination to one of the historic orders of ministry: deacons, priests, and bishops. There are also intentional leaders who serve the church in a trained and called capacity like youth ministry or administration. There is another form of leadership: the *accidental* leader. All humans find themselves in this type of leadership from time to time. It is experienced when we find ourselves called into a position to which we did not especially aspire and for which we were not trained. In the church, these leaders are found on outreach teams, leading church school or formation classes, serving on a committee, being the church treasurer or warden, or serving on the vestry.

So the basic distinction is that *intentional* leaders sought to be leaders in the context where they serve and *accidental* leaders are invited, appointed, or elected to a leadership position out of the context where they live, the community of the faithful.

The truth is that though some leaders are intentional and some are accidental, even those who have intentional leadership roles are not necessarily trained in the skills needed for the exercise of ministry in today's church. This book will explore leadership skills and functions that belong in a community of Christian practice, the local congregation. Such leadership finds its biblical foundation in Paul's words to one of the early, fledgling communities. Paul writes in Ephesians 4:12 that leaders are "to equip the saints for the work of ministry, for building up the body of Christ." This service is for the purpose of unity and the restoration of divine and human relationships, which is the missional purpose of the church.[1]

---

1. The catechism of the Episcopal Church teaches that the mission of the church is "to restore all people to unity with God and each other through Christ." Missional churches intentionally engage this restoration to which God is calling all the faithful and in which God is already active in the world.

Yes, some leaders have had extensive training for the position they hold. And yes, many never sought or had training for the position in which they serve. The larger truth is that the common ground all leaders share is baptism. It is that gift and grace that serves as the primary grounding for leadership in God's church. As every individual who is washed by those waters is different, so each one of the baptized offers that with which they have been uniquely blessed. These offerings, when combined, contribute a rich tapestry of leadership for the community of faith and its work in the world.

The intent of this book is to offer ideas, processes, and approaches that will build ministry and advance God's mission in your community, whether you are highly trained or surprised by being selected, whether you are an intentional or accidental leader.

Appreciation

Committing words to a page brings with it indebtedness to a long procession of people who have influenced and formed you along the way. After forty years as a priest in the church, my list is huge. If you know me, you are one of those people.

I feel it is important to name at least a few. The fact that this book has come to fruition is due in great part of the encouragement of my wife, Judy. Along with her I name my sons, Jonathan and Matthew, who have always been a source of enormous inspiration. I had the joy of serving as the long-term rector of Saint Alban's Parish in Hickory, North Carolina. Those dear people, especially the parish deacons, John Earl and Stewart Stoudemire, were the origin of and laboratory for many of the concepts developed in this book.

In the seven years before my retirement, I had the good fortune to serve alongside a young priest, the Rev. Alan Akridge, at Saint Alban's Church. Working with Alan was both challenging and creative. There is probably no sentence in this book that is without his influence.

Gratitude is also extended to those who offered their time and thought in reading an early version of the manuscript or exploring concepts with me that found their way into this book. They are Gary Coffey, Mike Cogsdale, Brian Cole, Robert Fain, Morgan Gardner, Elizabeth Whitten Jones, Francis King, Ron Kyle, Reggie McNeal, Tim McRee, Norma Robinson, Karla Woggon, and Dwight Zscheile, .

For you and all the saints, I am grateful.

Introduction

I live in the foothills of the Blue Ridge Mountains. Their ridges and valleys are beautiful, filled with majesty and awe. But they, and many mountain ranges, are in trouble. Many of our woodlands have become unhealthy and fragile. The causes are many. Acid rain has devastated the top of Mount Mitchell, the tallest mountain in the eastern United States. Blights have taken out whole species and are depleting others. Non-native plants, like our infamous southern kudzu, are taking over the space once occupied by indigenous trees and plants. These introductions have gradually changed the landscape. Over time the natural processes that evolved to create a healthy forest ecosystem have become compromised.

Fire, of course, is a natural process that causes a dramatic instant change. While we often think first of the devastating effects of fire on human life and personal property, those who have studied forest ecosystems have discovered that in many places fire is beneficial to the health of the forest. Fires are a natural process that can be not only advantageous but also necessary for the health of the system.

Though an area might look dead immediately after a fire, the vegetation that has turned to ash remains on the forest floor. Fire recycles the ash into nutrients to promote new plant growth. The blackened soil is rich in newly released minerals. In the soil are roots and stems and seeds that find ideal conditions in the warm, mineral-rich soil. In fact, there are some species that require fire to complete their reseeding.

In the last decades there has been a growing concern to manage forests in a way to create health and balance. These forestry practices now include the provision of allowing fires to burn so that unhealthy forests might be leveled and the rich nutrients in the soil released to nurture new, more vigorous life.

The church of God in the late twentieth and early twenty-first centuries may be likened to an unhealthy forest. For each century in our two-thousand-year history, the church has seen the introduction of institutional systems and dogmatic elaboration. There was a great "fire" called the Reformation five hundred years ago. The soil was replenished with nutrients and the institutional church (both Reformed and Catholic) was rerooted and, to some degree, at least in the rhetoric, a return to the more pristine nature of the early church sought.

Our culture—and the churches within it—is at a crucial and critical point in history. The church as an institution is stressed and unhealthy. The evidence is found in dwindling financial support, declining attendance, and the fear of both loss and change. These realities have descended like a pall on many of the faithful. We have before us a choice not unlike the one Moses presented to the people of Israel: "I have set before you life and death, blessings and curses. Choose life so that you and your descendants may live" (Deut. 30:19b).

> A sower went out to sow his seed; and as he sowed, some fell on the path and was trampled on. . . . Some fell on the rock. . . . Some fell among thorns. . . . Some fell into good soil, and when it grew, it produced a hundredfold. . . . as for that in the good soil, these are the ones who, when they hear the word, hold it fast in an honest and good heart, and bear fruit with patient endurance.
>
> —Luke 8:5-8, 15

Observers of the shift that is underway see patterns that compare it to the dramatic events of the Great Reformation. In fact, a frequent reference to the character and nature of this new experience is to call it a *new* Reformation. Hopefully, we are again engaging a beneficial fire[2] that releases nutrients and new growth.

The good news is that death was not the outcome five hundred years ago and death, while being stared in the face, is not the likely outcome of this new Reformation. Signs of life, of robust and godly change, are everywhere. Yes, God's people are facing heretofore unknown challenges, but decisions are being made (albeit slowly) to reform the old institution into a nimble, creative, mission-centric gathering of the people of God. This is the process of rerooting, of finding that which has lasting value, and using those seeds to grow the church: fresh, renewed, and robust.

The cultivation of leaders roots the congregation in ministry as it forms the people within the church and sends them out in mission to join God's purpose in the world. Great leaders are needed for this ministry, leaders who are focused, equipped, and collegial. These leaders become the nutrients needed by the soil to plant and participate in the extension of the reign of God in their neighborhood, town, region, and, ultimately, in the world.

While the primary purpose of this book is to assist members of the vestry in building the form and face of ministry in local congregations, any gathering

---

2. Fire is also the generative experience of the earliest followers of Jesus on the day of the descent of the Holy Spirit at Pentecost, the day the church was equipped with power from on high to engage the mission entrusted to them by Jesus. Resource F, "The Five Marks of Mission" (p. 104), in part two develops this concept more fully.

of leaders can use most of the ideas found in these pages. The church, though stressed, is rich in nutrients from our earliest days and new seed is ready for planting. May you find the tools within these pages helpful for your church's planting season. Our task is to provide rich soil, the best of seed, sunlight, and water while remembering that "God [gives] the growth" (1 Cor. 3:6).

The Shape of the Book

There are two parts to this book. The first part surveys ten attributes that are like the root system on a tree. When developed and operative, these functions lift the vestry beyond a group that meets for long sessions to worry about money or minding a list of building maintenance issues. As well, vestries have historically spent much time recruiting leaders and volunteers for various types of service in the church. Much of vestry activity is born out of a problem. How can we find someone to . . . ? Where is the money to . . . ? What can we do about . . . ? Who will help us with . . . ?

Each of the ten chapters in this book present not so much a checklist of steps to leadership but a broad selection of tools—approaches, gifts, and blessings—that create unique ways and means of making or keeping a congregation true to its purpose of revealing Christ in the community. As a result, the root system helps the tree grow to be strong, healthy, and giving. It grows not just for itself, but to be a contributor to the health of its environment.

Before we launch into the cultivation of vestries and leadership teams, there is an extended prologue that sets out to describe the environment in which the church[3] lives today. If rerooting and reseeding is the route we are taking, then we need to know that which we need to take from the past and plant in the soil of the twenty-first century. The prefix *re* means *again* or *return to a previous condition*. The prologue looks at our previous conditions. Over and over you will encounter the prefix *re* in this book. The reason is that virtually every challenge we encounter can be addressed by taking up existing DNA, blessing it, and refitting it for service in a new world. The good news wrapped in this truth is that the church already has everything it needs to be vital, resilient, and faithful in the twenty-first century. The prologue probes the source and evolution of our source code, our DNA.

---

3. Unless otherwise indicated, when "the church" is referenced in this book, it is referring to the church in the Western world, the church which has a significant inheritance of the faith mediated by and through Christendom. In other parts of the world—particularly Africa, Asia, and Latin America—Christianity is surging and thriving.

PROLOGUE
Setting the Context

The marks of centuries of construction (and sometimes deconstruction) of the institution we call church run deep on the shape and form of any local congregation, especially those connected to historic denominations in North America. Each expression of the church has found its own cherished doctrines and governance intended to serve the institutional shape of the church. These varying historical identities of the church formed the minds and hearts of God's people in particular ways over hundreds of years.

> The missional church represents God in the encounter between God and human culture. It exists not because of human goals or desires, but as a result of God's creating and saving work in the world.
>
> —The Gospel and Our Culture Network

How each particular tribe of Christians incarnate themselves in the world today has its curses and blessings. No specific brand of Christianity seems free of the growing distance people in the Western world are putting between themselves and most institutional expressions of Christianity.[4] For those inside the denominational church, the question of the twenty-first century becomes, like Dr. Phil's frequent refrain, "How's that working for you?" The apparent answer is "Not very well."

All the uncertainties and changes of an emerging age of ministry come to a head in the life of the local congregation. Once a stable center and guarantor of community and family life, it witnessed to the deep values and commitments that made life coherent and whole. Today, the local church has merely become one institution alongside all the others, competing for time and energy and often less sure than the others about its basic reason for being.[5]

---

4. Though beyond the scope of this book, it is worth noting that Christianity in the Eastern world and Global South is flourishing.

5. Loren Mead, *The Once And Future Church: Reinventing the Church for the New Mission Frontier* (Herndon, VA: Alban Institute, 1991), 40.

These are the words of Loren Mead, a prophet in these changing times, in the prophet's role of truth telling. His conclusion is based on an extensive study of the church through the ages. Since Mead's pioneering work, many have added to the discussion.

The communal life of God's people has taken shape in its interface with the context of its daily life. In earliest years, called the Apostolic Era, the church found itself in a hostile cultural and political context. For the first three hundred years of the church, there was a strong missional character among those who followed in the Way (Acts 9:2, 19:9). Their numbers grew in response to God's message of grace that each follower carried. The missionary enterprise of "going into the world" to participate in what God was doing belonged to all the baptized.

Organizationally the apostolic church was evolving, responding to its contextual need as seen in the appointment of the first deacons to serve the widows and orphans (Acts 6). The earliest leaders responded collegially to the circumstances, even offering variances for differing environments. Paul shaped the message for Gentiles and Peter carried it to the Jews. Gifts distributed among the followers of the Way were shared within the whole gathering of believers and used to strengthen the fellowship and open it to new believers.

In this formative era there were varying degrees of acceptance by the political and social spheres of life. Even in the face of opposition or in some cases possible martyrdom, Christians crossed any perceived boundaries to witness to the power of the faith they had found in Jesus Christ. That movement signaled a high level of commitment to carry the Good News into the world and cooperate with the movement of the Holy Spirit in the world.

Perhaps looking for a way to consolidate political power or perhaps for genuine spiritual reasons, in 313 CE, Constantine promulgated the Edict of Milan, establishing religious toleration in the Roman Empire. Legend has it that in the previous year, just before the Battle of the Milvian Bridge, Constantine saw a sign in the sky from the Christian God that promised victory. Upon achieving victory, he marched into Rome as the undisputed emperor. Perhaps looking for a coherent rallying principle for the citizens of the Roman Empire, Constantine began a process to make Christianity the official religion of the empire.

The benefit to the church was multifold. Confiscated properties were returned. Great edifices dedicated to the Christian God were erected. Clergy received privileges and the church was supported financially. The hostility between church and state was overcome with closer and more amicable relations. Since the Roman Empire was the seed of Western civilization, the church became woven into the empire's fabric.

The action inaugurated in 313 has come to be marked as the beginning of the Constantinian or Christendom era of the church.

Christendom Takes Hold

At its core, Christendom is a sociopolitical reality. With toleration granted in the early fourth century, Christianity became the established religion of the empire by the end of that century. In short order, Christianity became a defining characteristic of all lands where the empire extended. The kingdoms that evolved out of the Roman Empire planted their particular version of Christianity wherever they went to conquer and colonize.

The removal of persecution and the advent of official sanction allowed the church the freedom to build itself institutionally. Structure does not form *ex nihilo* (out of nothing). Over time, the seeds for the church's institutional growth were found in the body politic.

The primitive church, the Apostolic Era, had leadership that was organic, regional, and theologically diverse. To help organize the disparate parts of the faith, Constantine called the first Ecumenical Council, the Council of Nicea, creating a time-honored and collaborative way to build doctrinal consensus. The model might be somewhat parallel to a New England town meeting as all eighteen hundred bishops of the church were invited (though only about 10 or 15 percent attended). The large number of bishops for a relatively small segment of the population indicates how dispersed and truly local such oversight was in the apostolic church. Additionally, each bishop was invited to bring an entourage of priests and deacons. The first Ecumenical Council was, by design, highly representative of the entire church.

One of the features of this conclave was the adoption of universal church law (or as it is called in the church *canon law*). One cannot help but notice that institutionalization had already begun and that prominent bishoprics in prominent political centers evolved into places with elevated status. By the time of the second Ecumenical Council six decades later, the bishop of Rome, the political capital of the Empire, and the bishop of Constantinople, the new Rome, appeared to be gaining significant ascendency. It is not coincidental that bishops in political power centers begin to take on precedence and power.

The world of the empire was Christian and Christianity became a binding agent of the empire, and in later Christendom, civilization. This era may be viewed graphically as:[6]

THE CHRISTENDOM ERA
Third through Twentieth Centuries

Hostile/Pagan World Outside
The Domain of Missionaries

Empire/State Boundary = Church Boundary

Multiple Jurisdictions *

Local Parishes

Evolving Lines of Authority and Hierarchy
in place by High Middle Ages

In North America multiple jurisdictions (dioceses and state churches) evolved into denominations which overlapped geographically.

As Christianity took on official status, the barrier between the church and the world decreased and, eventually, disappeared.[7] The hostile environment was replaced by acceptance and, often, required adherence. The mission frontier was no longer outside one's doorstep; the frontier became the territory beyond the empire with specialists, called missionaries, sent to convert the heathen in those far-off lands.

---

6. The graphic representations of the Apostolic Era, Christendom Era, and post-Christendom Era are based on the work and illustrations of Loren Mead.

7. See an extended discussion by Loren Mead in the *Once and Future Church* series.

Local congregations came to be considered as geographical regions with membership defined by birth and the place one lived. Priests transformed into chaplains, holding forth the idea of citizenship with obedience to the state as normative. As the church gave its allegiance, the law of the land gave preferential treatment to the church and enforced Christian values. Gradually any distinction between religious and secular culture was blurred.

Being a good citizen, according to many who grew up in Christendom, is the same thing as being a good Christian. Mission, in this now receding paradigm of a Constantinian Church, was to carry the gospel to far-off lands, those places at the margins of Western civilization. The hierarchical structures that constitute and organize congregations and denominations today were largely conceived in and created to work within this Constantinian Era.

To engage what is now emerging, first look at the world of the Apostolic Era. It is the time of martyrs and careful incursion into the world with the message of Jesus Christ. The boundaries around the local gatherings of Christians are guarded, sometimes secret. Yet in this unfriendly environment the acts of mission with its good news of peace, reconciliation, and wholeness cause the church to grow spiritually and numerically.

First Three Centuries of the Church

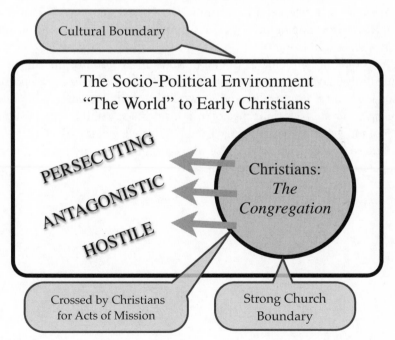

The dynamics of life as Christians, seen in the first several centuries of Christianity represented in the previous illustration, may now be compared to our present time and experiences as people of faith. The key feature (when laid alongside the early Apostolic Era of the church) is the return of the local gathering of Christians as a primary unit of mission in the church through the ministry of all the people of God.

The Context of the Church Today

A variety of language has been coined to describe the culture within which the church is currently living. Some of the language describes this hard-to-categorize era in "post" categories: post-Christian, post-Christendom, post-Constantinian, postmodern. These are good descriptors since we have a better of understanding of the past against the present or what we shall encounter in the future.

Mark Dyer, professor of theology and mission at Virginia Seminary and a retired bishop, takes a long view of that past and has pointed out to us humorously and profoundly, "About every five hundred years the church has a giant rummage sale." Then he adds wryly: "We're due." Picking up from Bishop Dyer, Phyllis Tickle, noting that the last giant rummage sale was the Reformation, names this new Reformation Era "The Great Emergence."[8] This era, it is noted, is emerging out of a previous paradigm of hierarchy, control, and a narrow sense of mission.

As people of faith emerge from a previous incarnation of the church (or, using Bishop Dyer's metaphor, work through a giant rummage sale), a possible outcome can be new vitality and growth. This is an exceedingly important principle to note. The church is not just in a death spiral. It is entering a time of profound change that, if engaged and not denied, will take the Good News forward to new generations of those who can find power and purpose among people who name themselves as Christian.

---

8. Phyllis Tickle, *The Great Emergence: How Christianity Is Changing and Why* (Grand Rapids: Baker Books, 2008).

The world into which this new form of church is emerging looks something like this:

THE EMERGING PARADIGM
The New Apostolic Era

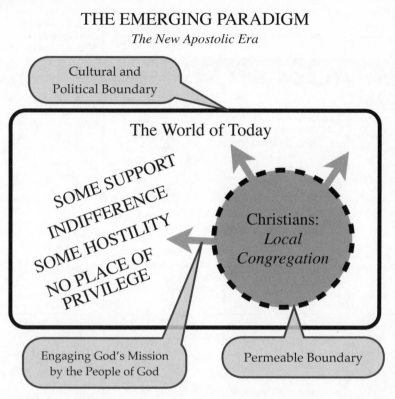

A definition of this emerging paradigm of post-Christendom is "the culture that emerges as the Christian faith loses coherence within a society that has been definitively shaped by the Christian story and as the institutions that have been developed to express Christian convictions decline in influence."[9] This reformation in our cultural environment is beginning to give shape and definition to change. We, in the Western world, live in transition from the Christendom "captivity" of the Church to the emerging New Apostolic Era. One of the most noteworthy rerooting experiences of the church in this new era is the return of mission as the responsibility of all the people of God in their daily life.[10] In fact, mission is such a significant part of this newly emerging paradigm that some are calling it a Missional Era.

---

9. Stuart Murray, *Post-Christendom: Church and Mission in a Strange New World* (Carlisle, PA: Paternoster, 2004), 19.

10. See chapter 6 for further discussion of the Missional Era.

Putting the three eras of the church together, a simple chart might compare them in the following way:

THE THREE ERAS	Apostolic Church	Constantinian/ Christendom Church	New Apostolic Church [Post-Christendom]
Time Frame	Christ to 3/400 AD	400 AD to 1900s	Present
Environment or Context	Larger society clearly hostile to Christians. Illegal. Culture and Christianity are at odds.	With Constantine, Christianity becomes both legal and the established religion. Society considers it good and normal to be Christian. Church and State united.	Society at best indifferent to church; at worse, antagonistic. Being Christian is a choice, but not necessarily popular. Symbiotic relationship with society ending.
Nature of Christian Community	Tightly knit, committed, dedicated, somewhat difficult to enter group.	State considered to be Christian, so whole "civilized" world is understood to be part of faith community. Small group does work and majority observe (or not).	Congregation again becomes the "working unit" of faith. Commitment and dedication again begin to define membership.
Mission	Very clear understanding of the call of EACH Christian to live out, witness, and share their faith with others in their personal lives in context of community.	As society becomes "Christian," mission seen as "out there" (pagan lands), done by "expert" missionaries on behalf of church.	Frontier of mission is, like the Apostolic Era, seen as significantly local. Every Christian is again seen as directly participating in God's mission, both locally and globally.
Clergy and Laity	Gifts and function related to "call" in community. Little sense of hierarchy with power over people.	Distinction between clergy and laity grows with increasing power to clergy; prestige and responsibility vested in clergy.	Clergy role again increasingly defined in terms of mentoring, training, supporting and encouraging; members are missional leaders, dedicated and faithful.

These basic paradigmatic shifts[11] thread their way throughout this book. Next, we turn to some of the institutions that may need some reinvention for the church and its leadership to be vital in the twenty-first century and

_____

11. There is a discussion of these movements and shifts in part two. See resource A on page 75.

beyond. As perceptive as those who are interpreting the present environment of the church can be, the insight offered is limited by a short span of accumulated history and evidence. There is much yet to be learned. But with this caveat declared, the movement of the Holy Spirit has brought much into the light and the church need not wait for the certainty of hindsight. To tarry is to lose opportunity.[12]

12. If you would like to dig more deeply into the nature and consequences of the shift, see Stanley Hauerwas and William H. Willimon's *Resident Aliens* (Nashville: Abingdon Press, 1989). See also Mike Regele's *Death of the Church* (Grand Rapids, MI: Zondervan, 1996). One of the earliest considerations of the mission of the church is found in Roland Allen's *The Spontaneous Expansion of the Church* (Eugene, OR: Wipf & Stock, 1997). The seminal study for the church in North America is Loren B. Mead's *The Once and Future Church* three-book series.

PART ONE

CHAPTER 1
A Reordered Path of
GOVERNANCE

In 2011, the Presiding Bishop of the Episcopal Church, Katharine Jefferts Schori, used a stark phrase when speaking to the church's Executive Council. She said we were in danger of committing "suicide by governance." Later in her remarks, Jefferts Schori said, "We need a system that is more nimble, that is more able to respond to change," calling for "a more responsive and adaptable and less rigid set of systems."[13]

As the church evolved, it took on more and more of the marks of an institution. Structures and rules were put in place to govern the behavior of those who banded together in congregations. This evolution was often marked with a movement from simplicity to greater and greater complexity. In Acts 6 we have the story the church uses to support the ordination of deacons. There was a need and in short order the apostles set apart seven men to minister to the need. Today the path to ordination as a deacon, be it a vocational deacon or a deacon who is preparing for ordination to the priesthood, is complex and elaborate.

Take any process that the local, diocesan, or national expression of church engages over time and the normal track is that the processes move more and more in the direction of complexity and regulation.[14] In the governance function of the vestry, it is helpful that all process be as nimble, responsible, and as useful as possible. Remember the axiom "keep it simple"? The best approach is often the most straightforward and simple path.

---

13. Mary Frances Schjonberg, "Presiding Bishop Warns Executive Council of 'Suicide by Governance,'" Episcopal News Service (Oct. 24, 2010).

14. This is true in virtually every human process, not just the church!

Some, perhaps much, of the vestry's encounter with inherited governing processes might not be, as yet, nimble and responsive. It is necessary to consider what the church's laws, called *canons*, expect and how vestries honor their responsibility. Leadership bodies who are rerooting themselves to be effective in this new age are finding ways to honor the important truth conveyed in the law by returning to or discovering ways that are more straightforward and less cumbersome. Keeping on the simple path in canonical responsibilities will become a trait with transferable usefulness in general vestry discussions.

Though there may be local or diocesan variances in governing law, vestries are "selected,"[15] according to the national canons, to tend to the temporal (or worldly) affairs of the church alongside the clergy who are to tend to the spiritual affairs of the church. This distinction is clean only on paper. In reality, both worldly and spiritual things are the concern of all leaders.

The worldly functions include tending the buildings and grounds, maintaining proper stewardship of all funds, stewarding annual giving and spending, making reports to the diocese and governmental entities, care of the temporal needs of a rector (or equivalent), auditing all financial and physical assets at least annually, and, when necessary, calling a new rector or vicar. The vestry is also responsible for keeping and preserving the minutes of its meetings; this is normally designated to a secretary or clerk. The vestry is the legal representative of the congregation.

Any of these actions that can, should be delegated to others who have a special calling or expertise. The vestry gratefully receives their gifts of time and talent, and then takes necessary action. In doing so the vestry utilizes a classic Anglican bit of wisdom called "subsidiarity." A simple definition is that the vestry takes on only those tasks that cannot be performed effectively by others. An example is having a person skilled in finances manage an audit or bookkeeping or cost estimating, and report to the vestry for any needed action. When delegated, the vestry should trust the person(s) to whom the ministry has been entrusted.

The vestry in its governing responsibility is accountable for compliance with all applicable rules and regulations. These include the national canons (laws) of the Episcopal Church, the canons and policies of the diocese, and the bylaws and formal or informal policy of the local congregation. So that these responsibilities do not surprise anyone who serves on a vestry, an annual review of all governing rules should be engaged by the vestry, normally upon

---

15. Note well that the word used for choosing members of the vestry in our national canons is *selected*. This word use is intentional. Vestries have canonical permission to explore many options of bringing leaders to service as members of the vestry.

the seating of new members.[16] These principles should be readily available at any meeting.

In general, the overtly governmental functions should claim only a *small* minority of the vestry's meeting time. If governance does consume excessive time, discipline yourselves to spend more time with the functions in chapters 2 through 10 in this book. It may be helpful to appoint someone as a process observer to monitor meetings and time discussions in order to bring all vestry work into balance. "A congregation easily becomes an end in its own mind—recruiting people to an empty discipleship of committee service, finance, and building maintenance. Institutional maintenance is a necessary, but ultimately secondary, function of a congregation. If souls are not transformed and the world is not healed, the congregation fails no matter what the treasurer reports."[17]

> Whoever wishes to be great among you must be your servant, and whoever wishes to be first among you must be your slave.
>
> —Matthew 20:26b–27

If the vestry is not a board of directors managing the temporal affairs and keeping the rules and regulations as a primary function, what should a vestry be? Beyond the governance of a congregation lies the larger horizon of where God is calling those in your faith community as they are formed as disciples of Jesus Christ. Congregations are unique and gifted collections of people endowed with abilities and talents that, when aggregated, offer God both voice and hands to accomplish the ongoing work of making whole that which is broken.

The major work of the vestry, which transforms governance into a generative, sense-making experience, is to create a frame of reference through which leaders process all governing issues and challenges. The output of such a process both builds health in individual members and energizes a congregation to move forward with growing capacity for participation in the reign of God.

Much of the time the vestry spends together has this purpose: How do we make God present in our families, our neighborhood, our town, and our world? As the vestry discerns its own unique answer to this question, it opens the ministry to everyone while helping to create a meaningful path through the complex adaptive changes every community needs to negotiate.

———

16. A suggestion: in advance of this discussion give each member a succinctly worded document that contains all governing rules.

17. Dan Hotchkiss, *Governance and Ministry: Rethinking Board Leadership* (Herndon, VA: Alban Institute, 2004), Kindle Edition 477–79.

Two Kinds of Change

Saint Dunstan's Church[18] is above average in size for an Episcopal church. It has about one hundred worshippers on Sunday. This has been true for about a decade, but twenty years ago the number was twice that. During that earlier period, the church had a rector, an associate, a part-time youth minister, and a director of Christian education. Now, they have one priest and volunteer leaders in youth ministry and Christian education.

Located in a suburban area of a small city, Saint Dunstan's has a small amount of capital debt from a Christian education wing built about the time attendance began to drop. Thinking that the church was no longer appealing to families with children, a building dedicated to the education of children and youth was intended to "fix the problem." However, young families have not made Saint Dunstan's their church home. The new wing is now mostly vacant on Sundays and in need of some minor repairs.

The twelve members of the vestry meet monthly in a corner of their parish hall. They open with prayer, approve the minutes, listen to a budget report, and resume what they believe to be a never-ending discussion. The repairs needed on the education wing surface again. "Do we need to have a rummage sale to help pay for repairs?" "Where are the kids it was built for?" "Why aren't we attracting new folks, especially younger members?" "Maybe we need to hire a part-time youth minister or something."

In the midst of this discussion another wrinkle is added. "Visitors don't feel welcome here. I invited a coworker a month ago and she came when I wasn't here. No one spoke to her." Problem solving sets in. "Let's train our greeters better." "Maybe the rector needs to make a bolder welcoming announcement." "I think the rector should be visiting more people, at least that is what some parishioners have said to me. She spends too much time in her office."

After two hours, the meeting adjourns. Most members are exhausted and no solutions seemed to be put forth. The issues will be revisited at the next meeting.

The real resolution to the situation is the purpose of this book. It is important to note one dynamic here before moving on. The place where the vestry is stuck has to do with change. Change comes in two kinds: technical change and adaptive change.[19]

Technical change is familiar to everyone. We encounter problems and circumstances for which there is a known remedy. When our faucet leaks in the

---

18. "Saint Dunstan's Church" is a composite of several Episcopal churches.

19. For an extended discussion of adaptive and technical change, see Ronald A. Heifetz and Marty Linsky, *Leadership on the Line* (Boston: Harvard Business School Press, 2002).

bathroom, we call a plumber. The inculcated reaction in most of us is to seek a technical change when we are faced with a problem. Our default inclination is to fix the problem. This is the realm of *management* as opposed to *leadership*.

Adaptive change is about learning new ways, changing attitudes, remodeling behaviors, and broadening our values. Without engaging adaptive change, many of the problematic experiences we have will go unresolved and, over the long term, fester. Adaptive change is about changing us, changing processes, changing our lives. Probably the most common source of leadership failure is the temptation to treat challenges with a technical fix rather than employ the longer, harder work of adaptive change.

Saint Dunstan's was using technical change when adaptive change was needed. The good news for Saint Dunstan's is that their rector attended a diocesan study day for clergy. She came back with an *aha* moment to share with the vestry. There was no overnight cure, but with the help of a nearby Presbyterian minister who was schooled in change theory, they began to break out of their cycle of limitation and lament.

RESOURCES

See a fuller description of subsidiarity in "The Principle of Subsidiarity" in the resource section (p. 91).

There is a suggested Order of Meeting (agenda) in "Vestry Meetings" on p. 81 of the resource section.

QUESTIONS

What do you think the Presiding Bishop could have been saying to your church when she said that the church was in danger of committing "suicide by governance"?

Do you know your diocesan canons on vestries? Are you in compliance? Do you have parish bylaws or customs that need adjustment?

A board of directors has become a frequently used analogy for a church vestry. How does it help or hurt to refer to a vestry in this way?

CHAPTER 2
Cultivating Health through
MODELING

Let your minds be filled with everything that is true, everything that is honorable, everything that is upright and pure, everything that we love and admire, with whatever is good and praiseworthy. –Philippians. 4:8 (NJB)

Before the great shift presently underway in the church, many church leaders had as their primary responsibility to grow the institution of the church. Many of those who have taken up leadership in the postmodern, new Apostolic Era church are in the process of refocusing their attention on helping spiritual people grow. Leaders are becoming appropriately aware of modeling a growing faith life so that it might be replicated in others. The experience of the shift is that growth is not about increasing the institutional balance sheet of membership and budgets but about faith and how we plan, model, and witness.

> Show yourself in all respects a model of good works, and in your teaching show integrity, gravity, and sound speech that cannot be censured; then any opponent will be put to shame, having nothing evil to say of us.
>
> —Titus 2:7-8

A leader who models the way sets an example by setting in place behavior and expressed attitudes that are consistent with the shared faith and values of the people of God. Leading by example is a way to make tangible the core values and vision of the church. The people of God watch leaders to see if there is congruence between what leaders say and what they do.

Leaders model the way forward as they engage in specific practices:

- Set aside time to involve themselves in expressing positive core values that are demonstrable in their behavior.
- Take advantage of teachable moments to point out the lived expression of what the church holds in regard.
- Continuously collect stories that demonstrate the congregation's values for use later when they are given opportunities to hold them up before the people.
- Ask questions that drive the thoughts of parishioners back to vision and value reference points.
- Ensure that symbols are strategically placed that represent the church's core principles and values, such as posting the Vestry Covenant (see chap. 7).
- Measure and tell experiences that are directly tied to the congregation's values, like feeding the hungry. What you measure is what you value.
- Make it a point to praise those who exemplify positive principles.[20]

When leaders model the way, they demonstrate that they not only show up and pay attention but also participate in the process of making extraordinary things happen.

All who serve as leaders bring with them unique skills and experiences. When these are amassed into a leadership group like a vestry, it can, at least in the beginning, be somewhat discordant. The person who manages as a profession wants to manage on the vestry, the person who teaches wants to teach, a president wants to preside, and a worker wants to get the job done. Then mix in personalities: introverts and stoics, relaxed and deeply feeling people. And top off this mix with the varying perspectives of generations.

To be sure, the vestry is a microcosm of the local congregation. The congregation may be too great a collection of humanity to work with as a whole, but vestries present a group small enough to work through challenges toward healthy communication and practice. As members of the vestry model the way to a common ministry, the principles they use filter into the congregation. By way of the vestry's modeling function, the tone of parish life gently moves toward the positive example being set by its leaders. Proper modeling can have the desired effect of defusing conflictual behaviors, feelings of being stuck, and energy-draining lack of focus.

The modeling function of a leader creates a common platform upon which all may stand while honoring the rich diversity and contributions of every

---

20. This list is derived from the work of James M. Kouzes and Barry Z. Posner in their book, *The Leadership Challenge* (San Francisco: Jossey-Bass, 2008).

person.[21] There are principles and practices that model congregational life at its best. The discipline known as Appreciative Inquiry is capable of offering a common place to stand and lead. As well, Appreciative Inquiry offers the members of the vestry, its officers, and the clergy a means to model vigorous, constructive leadership in the congregation. Significantly, use of this appreciative discipline puts leadership in an adaptive change mode and pushes technical change into proper use in cases where appropriate.

Instead of focusing on problems, shortcomings, and deficiencies, Appreciative Inquiry looks for what is healthy and life giving. Upon discovery of where the congregation is at its best, the endeavor becomes one of enhancing and expanding those points and places of vitality. The new thing leaders are asked to model is the ability to shift their focus on problems. Note well: shedding problem fixing as a central approach to life is hard work! The payoff is significant since Appreciative Inquiry's approach gives leaders a tool for deep, spiritual discernment.

This chart compares a problem-solving approach with the appreciative way.

TRADITIONAL PROCESS	APPRECIATIVE INQUIRY
Define the problem	Search for solutions that already exist
Fix what's broken	Amplify what is working
Focus on decay	Focus on life-giving forces
What are the problems?	What is working well?

This is only an overview of the process; it is not a full explanation of Appreciative Inquiry. You will find more discussion of Appreciative Inquiry in chapter 9 and in the resource section. The core message for leaders honoring the modeling function is to present from a healthy, positive spirit. Jesus put it this way: "I came that (you) may have life, and have it abundantly" (John 10:10b).

The circumstance that Jesus speaks to is our human penchant to go in negative directions, to focus on scarcity or things broken. His witness is that the purpose of God's presence among us is to move us toward abundance, toward

---

21. To make your modeling function robust, it is important that you seek a diverse vestry. Consider the use of a nominating committee to present a slate for election at your annual meeting. The presentation of a slate of nominees allows for balance and diversity: newer parishioners and long-time members, men and women, young and old, quiet and gregarious. The governing law (canons) allows this approach by use of the word *selection* to bring new members to the vestry. Your diocese may have a more narrow approach; work within their guidelines or seek a variance from your bishop.

the positive, toward appreciation. Consider the impact on any congregation when leaders model appreciation and abundance.

Remember, if you accept the challenge to move away from being a "fixer," you relinquish any effort to fix other people. When you accept the leadership function of being a model, the focus for change is you. The question becomes: "Am I modeling the kind of leadership I would want from those who lead me?" People will not engage that which you are not modeling yourself.

❧

In a young church with limited resources and in the midst of constructing their first building, Edna, a parishioner who served as a nurse in the local college's infirmary, noticed a need in the community. At the soup kitchen where she served from time to time, her diagnostic skills kicked in as she observed people go through the line to get lunch. All she could see were medical needs. After entering into conversation with individuals, Edna's diagnosis was confirmed. Person after person told her stories of their limited access to medical care.

So what did Edna do? She prayed and prayed some more.

When she felt like she had received some direction from the Lord, Edna called together a group to discern with her how God's people might respond to the need. In this small group was a doctor on his way to becoming a deacon, an accountant on his way to becoming a priest, and a parishioner with a heart for caring for people on the margins.[22] They met and met again. The idea they developed was a screening clinic for those in need of medical care, with the hope of connecting serious medical cases for *pro bono* services in the medical community. But after the concept began to come into focus, what they kept seeing were limitations. The church had no spare funds. There was no place to house this clinic. They had no medical equipment.

The turning point that led this team to model possibility was lying on the side of a road one morning. A local physician was moving to another city. He put an old examination table on the side of the road to be picked up by the sanitation department. The doctor on Edna's team saw it and asked for it. The turn was made. From then on the team saw opportunities rather than problems.

The soup kitchen had an unused room in its storefront location. Doctors began to donate supplies. Bits and pieces of things useful and needful arrived. Those with nursing and medical skills offered their time. The shoestring medical clinic opened its doors during lunch at the soup kitchen. As time pro-

---

22. The cofounders of the Good Samaritan Medical Clinic in Hickory, North Carolina, are Edna Lewis, RN, Susan Coleman, the Reverend John Earl, MD, and the Reverend Bert Eaton. The clinic is now part of the Greater Hickory Cooperative Christian Ministry, a consortium of over seventy churches in the community.

gressed, more and more gifts of supplies and skills were offered. Edna's little dream became a big reality as they moved from scarcity to abundance. God, indeed, was moving and this group found its way forward.

Along the way, the clinic grew in its ability to serve the unemployed and uninsured. Today, three decades later, the clinic has a budget of $600,000 and is staffed by 138 physicians, nurses, technicians, aides, and volunteers. The little screening clinic at the soup kitchen has transformed into a full-service clinic offering a pharmacy, an eye clinic, a dental clinic, and a diabetes education center in a state-of-the-art facility offering $15 million in free services annually to those in need.

Scarcity, indeed, has turned to abundance and a community is being served by faith that was once the size of a mustard seed. The founders modeled their confidence that possibility can become reality.

RESOURCE

See "Appreciative Inquiry Primer" (p. 93), as well as a visual overview of both Traditional Problem-Solving and Appreciative Inquiry approaches (pp. 96–97) in the resource section.

QUESTIONS

Have you made the shift from an institutional model, from growth in numbers to growth in faith?

How do you model appreciative, abundant attitudes in your life? How does the vestry utilize nondeficit approaches to its ministry?

Gather for a storytelling time and share stories of when your church experienced a move from scarcity to abundance. Who was involved? What was it about? What was the turning point for you? What energy was present then that might be accessed today?

CHAPTER 3
New Roots through
COLLABORATION

We are better individually and collectively when we reason and pray together. Vestry members and clergy are at their best when they collaborate. The new era in which we live notes that strict, hierarchical command-and-control systems are brittle and collapsing. Lines of authority that formerly were represented in pyramidal organizational charts are being erased in favor of simpler, relational connections. This relational connection is known as *networking*.

The primitive church, with its close, connectional, organic sinews, had a powerful understanding of collaboration and connections. Saint Paul, to whom most of the Christian Scriptures are attributed, affirms this in "body" language. "Indeed, the body does not consist of one member but of many. . . . God arranged the members in the body, each one of them, as he chose. If all were a single member, where would the body be? As it is, there are many members, yet one body. . . . The members may have the same care for one another. If one member suffers, all suffer together with it; if one member is honored, all rejoice together with it. Now you are the body of Christ and individually members of it" (1 Cor. 12:14, 18–20, 25–27).

The practice of decision making by consensus as a group process is an important element in recapturing the vitality of that Apostolic Era. As the vestry learns this godly skill/gift and shares in this process, collaborative discernment will become the preferred form of decision making throughout the church's teams, groups, and committees. And it doesn't stay within the church. When people learn the value of this form of decision making, they take it with them into the world.

> What I do you cannot do; but what you do, I cannot do. The needs are great, and none of us, including me, ever do great things. But we can all do small things, with great love, and together we can do something wonderful.
>
> —Mother Teresa

Consensus is formed by a thorough discussion of the issue at hand. Along the way, any member of the vestry may put forth that which he or she believes to be the corporate mind of the vestry on the matter as a proposed "consensus statement of the vestry." If agreement is found, a consensus statement is recorded in the minutes as the agreed will of the vestry. If not, there is further listening required and a restatement needs to seek the right balance.

On some issues, consensus will be hard to achieve, but the effort will be worthwhile and uniting. If consensus cannot be formed on a matter, decision making on that particular issue is deferred to an agreed-upon later date. At that gathering (no more than thirty days later), the vestry re-engages the issue, reminding each other that it is God's will that they be of one mind, not necessarily of one opinion. The key is that all are heard and their nuanced concerns and thoughts are taken seriously.

It should be noted that persons have the right, *initially*, to stand alone. One person or a few people may hold truth for all. No one should be compelled to join the majority in an attempt to force consensus. There is no forced unity in consensus formation. Likewise, those holding single opinions should not use this right to prevent movement toward a decision.

Consensus actually transcends voting and winners/losers/majorities/minorities. The process is actually about *hearing* our brothers and sisters. A consensus is achieved when the vestry makes a statement all can accept as the mind of the vestry. Note well: The statement may not be the personal opinion of individual members, but rather a position an individual can *accept* as a position of the vestry. The good of the community takes ascendency in the end; individual opinions are fully and completely expressed in the formative stages of consensus.

Once declared, however, *all* persons are morally bound to completely support the decision. If a member of the vestry cannot work with consensus formation, their gifts might better be used elsewhere in parish life. Consensus formation on a vestry or in a leadership group requires a significant level of maturity in those who serve as leaders.

In addition to consensus formation, there is another useful tool that assists collaboration in a congregation. The process is called *mapping*.[23] The truth behind this process is parallel to the truth behind Appreciative Inquiry—God is a God of abundance and blessing. In this simple exercise everyone writes on sticky notes a blessing, gift, connection, or ability (referred to as an "asset") that they are willing to give to God through the church. With prompts from a leader a group—small or large—writes down (for example) twenty assets. If you

---

23. Luther Snow, *The Power of Asset Mapping: How Your Congregation Can Act on Its Gifts* (Herndon, VA: Alban Institute, 2004).

have one hundred people in the room, you will have two thousand assets. Placing these on tables or walls, you can group gifts in affinity circles. Everyone can go to the wall and group together a set of assets for an instant work plan to serve God's mission through the church.

Here is an example: The people of Saint James Church gathered in their parish hall. Each was asked to write down twenty assets on sticky notes. From a wall filled with notes the following assets or gifts were assembled: *I bake cookies. I am a nurse. I am a good organizer. I speak Spanish. I am in marketing. I like children. I like people. I have some used medical equipment. I am a nurse practitioner.* It had already been noted that the church owned an empty building downtown and wanted to put it to some good use. In a manner of moments the group had created an idea for a blood pressure clinic for Spanish-speaking migrant workers in the empty building, offering child supervision, cookies for hospitality, a greeter, an organizer, and someone who knew how to get the word out. *Voila*: instantaneous collaborative mission.

RESOURCE

For an asset-mapping primer, see "Introduction to Asset-Based Ministry" (p. 98) in the resource section.

DISCUSSION

Do you use decision making by consensus? If so, do you find that advantageous? If not, what might it bring to your vestry decisions?

How do you practice hearing what God is offering for the good of the body in your congregation and for the good of the world through your congregation?

Every congregation is richly blessed with parishioners who have gifts (assets) to offer. How do you access these gifts now? How might the asset-mapping process serve you?

CHAPTER 4
Cultivating Leaders as
CHAMPIONS

A champion is one who supports a cause. It is the nature of any leader to have a passion for one or more particular facets of the life of a congregation. An example in Scripture is the story of David and Goliath (1 Sam. 17). Goliath was a giant warrior who was the champion of the Philistines. Little David became the reluctant champion of the Israelites. The word *champion* literally means the "man between the two" or "mighty man." In both Goliath and David we have leaders who stand up for the interests of their constituency. It is worth noting that in the biblical story passion defeats size and skill.

> The strong leader does whatever they can to encourage and champion their team to become stronger themselves. The leader's task is to create the energy and vision where others might flourish.
> —Peter Drucker

For us the role of champion is being willing to stand up for an idea, an ideal, or a change. This champion helps keep proper focus on the discerned shared vision of a particular collaborative ministry or a discerned missional engagement with God's work in the community. Champions help find the right people and resources to apply for the fulfillment of a vision or change. Champions are the most important ingredients, besides God, for successful, healthy, collaborative ministry. Without a champion or team of champions in a local church, it will be difficult for your church to foster effective involvement.

Here are some profile characteristics of champions. Keep in mind that no human has all of these.

- knows how to be accountable
- models servanthood as life's rudder and is marked by humility
- is a creative collaborator

- knows how to cast a vision and recruit others to that vision
- is motivated by God's grace
- has God at the center of life
- can initiate, delegate, and communicate
- is involved in the life of the local congregation
- can handle challenge, ambiguity, and uncertainty

It would be helpful to conceive of the vestry (or any mission/ministry group) as a team of champions. Think of the health-generating possibilities of each member of the vestry championing a facet of the congregation's life together. Real discernment is needed to help leaders gravitate toward ministries for which they have some passion. When vestry members serve out of a champion role, their energy is enhanced and their abilities are utilized.

Simply dividing the ministry workload by the number of the members of the vestry and assigning each vestry member a category (like education, stewardship, finance, or buildings) guarantees uneven and often mediocre attentiveness. This has become the typical division of labor on vestries in the late twentieth century.

An alternative is to encourage champions being raised up to provide leadership. This type of passionate leadership will not arrive every January when you distribute or assign vestry responsibilities. There will likely be folks on the vestry who are passionate for a particular area of ministry. There are more in the congregation. Patience is urged as you let the Spirit do its work. Ultimately, champions will arise for every needed ministry. It may mean that some areas of ministry may not have a leader for a season, but letting some area lie fallow is a good biblical concept for renewal. Further, letting a ministry area go unattended can determine its value to the congregation. If the ministry is useful, the vacuum will draw out someone to lead, or if not, perhaps the time for that ministry has passed.

❧

A two-hundred-year-old church found a champion in Madeline, a five-year-old girl. The nursery at All Saints Church in Portsmouth, Ohio, was so worn and dated that some thought the toys might have been there since the first service in the church. The attention of the leaders was more on the adult stuff—updating the bathrooms and repainting the choir room. Richelle Thompson says:

> It was a surprise to learn that our five-year-old daughter had organized a bake sale to raise money to buy new toys for the nursery. She had made the rounds at coffee hour and had a sign-up list of treats to bring. She made signs—"Bake Sale 4 Kids"—and hung them around the church. She recruited other kids to help,

called the adults the week before the sale to remind them, and made cookies with her grandma as her offering.

On the morning of the bake sale, Madeline directed the placement of tables and arranged the items for sale. If anyone missed the sale table, Madeline would seek them out and offer them an opportunity to help buy toys for the nursery. From the eighty people in attendance, five hundred dollars was raised. Following the sale, a nursery committee was formed and Madeline was made a member. More contributions arrived and nursery priorities were set.

With Madeline as chief consultant, the committee commissioned a mural for the wall, purchased new toys, and secured pagers to alert parents. Rochelle concludes, "Led by the determination of children to have their place in church, we celebrated the new nursery with cookies and milk."

God will give the church everything it needs to fulfill its purpose.

RESOURCE

There is a fine discussion of the role of champion in Ori Brafman and Rod Beckstrom, *The Starfish and the Spider: The Unstoppable Power of Leaderless Organizations* (New York: Penguin Group, 2006). It is highly recommended. This book also teases out another function that is presented in chapter 5 of this book.

DISCUSSION

How has each member of your team served as a champion in life? In church?

How might your team or vestry harness the power of being a champion as a group of people? As individuals?

Children and youth are a blessing to the church. How is it that you champion their needs, gifts, and desires?

CHAPTER 5
Raising Up and Tapping the
CATALYSTS

Champions take on a need with conviction and personal engagement. Their passion and conviction carry them through the discernment of a new future. One of their characteristics is that they remain engaged as the new mission or ministry is implemented. An allied function to the champion is that of the catalyst. This function tracks differently but draws on similar gifts and abilities.

In contrast to a champion who immerses himself or herself into a specific process that carries the people of God forward as they engage in ministry and mission, the catalyst sets a process in motion but does not enter into the full implementation. What they offer is inspiration and encouragement. As the movement takes hold, they step aside to allow the process to take on a life of its own.

The gifts offered by a catalyst are to generate good ideas, cede control to leaders who are raised up, and provide inspiration that encourages action by others. The characteristics of a catalyst, which are somewhat similar to the characteristics of a champion, are:

> A basic premise of chemistry is that a catalyst forms a reaction which allows two or more substances to take on characteristics beyond their original capacities alone. People who serve as a leadership catalyst enable others to become more than they are capable of becoming by themselves.

- a demonstrated passion for the vision/project/change
- being grounded, with a healthy understanding of process
- the ability to tolerate open-endedness and ambiguity
- being trusting and collaborative
- faithfulness and emotional maturity
- the ability to let go

- the heart of a servant
- the ability to lead by example

Each of Julie Andrews's characters in *The Sound of Music* and *Mary Poppins* enter a dysfunctional family system, teach the members harmony and cooperation, show everyone healthy ways to get along, and sing happy songs. But Maria stays in the Von Trapp family while Mary Poppins pops out of town. In letting go of her leadership role, Mary Poppins transfers responsibility and ownership—the work of a catalyst. Rather than staying around for a celebration of her great work, she just flies away.

Mary Poppins, as a catalyst, brought an eclectic set of skills along with her outrageous enthusiasm and optimism for the tasks at hand. Her adaptability allowed her to bring creativity and innovation to the family. Significantly, she was connected to a vast network of human resources.[24]

This discussion has focused on the function of an individual who serves as a catalyst. There can be a collective expression of the function by the vestry or any leadership group. When the vestry operates as a catalyst, it creates the environment for healthy change processes directed toward mission, gets the process going, and then recedes to let the life of the new (or renewed) ministry or mission move out on its own leadership and charter.

> The most effective leader is one who can create the conditions by which he will actually lose his leadership.
>
> —Carl Rogers, Nobel laureate and psychologist

Actually, the catalyst function exercised by the vestry as a whole can become a regular practice. The leaders who serve on the vestry are reminded that their service is interim in nature (probably three years or less) and that exercising their catalytic ability raises up leaders for the longer haul. The ministers in the local congregation are, by the gift and grace of baptism, every person in the church. The function of serving as a catalyst builds this understanding and capacity as it raises up people with abilities and passion to lead a particular mission or ministry. "The priesthood of all believers," the great truth held high by Martin Luther, is nurtured and nourished when leaders stir up collaboration, encouragement, and release of control.

The roles of catalyst and champion serve a vital function for the church of today and tomorrow. As the church moves in a more intentionally missional way, space will be created for the ministry of catalysts and champions. Missional leaders watch for those who are showing evidence of being catalysts and champions. These gifts happen not only within official leadership circles but also in the wider community. When someone outside of designated leadership

---

24. The examples of Mary Poppins and Maria Von Trapp are from Ori Brafman and Rod Beckstrom's *The Starfish and the Spider*.

is a positive catalyst and champion, you may have been shown a future leader. Cultivate him or her. A good way to start is to apprentice those with leadership potential to known leaders for mentoring and formation.

RESOURCE

As with the role of champion, there is a discussion of the role of catalyst in the book *The Starfish and the Spider* by Ori Brafman and Rod Beckstrom.

DISCUSSION

The images of Mary Poppins and Maria Von Trapp help distinguish the roles of catalyst and champion. Do you have examples from your own experience?

Who do you know on the vestry who has the skills of being a catalyst? Who in your church? What is it that you notice about people when this skill is being used?

Name some areas of your life together that might benefit from the ministry of a catalyst.

CHAPTER 6
The Way Forward in
MISSION

"Go therefore and make disciples of all nations, . . . teaching them to obey everything I have commanded you. And remember, I am with you always . . ."
—Matthew 28:19–20

The Great Commission declares the "sent" character of the church. Mission is not just one function or program among many; *it is God's prime purpose for the church.* "It is not the Church of God that has a mission in the world, but the God of mission who has a Church in the world."[25] This powerful truth is often spoken by the Archbishop of Canterbury.

This re-rooting of the church in its apostolic DNA has its genesis in the middle of the twentieth century. Karl Barth writes:

> The church is the only organisation in the world that exists solely for the benefit of its non-members.
>
> —William Temple (1881–1944)
> Archbishop of Canterbury

> "God so loved"–not the Christian, but–"the world." "I am the light of the world," says the Lord, and by His own self-giving He passes the light on to His disciples: "Ye are the light of the world!" . . . How extraordinary the Church's preaching, teaching, ministry, theology, political guardianship and missions would be, how it would convict itself of unbelief in what it says, if it did not proclaim to all men that God is not against man but for man. It need not concern itself with the "No" that must be said to human presumption and human sloth. This "No" will be quite audible enough when as the real Church it concerns itself with the washing of feet and nothing else. This is the obedience which it owes to its Lord in this world.[26]

---

25. This quote is attributed to both Tim Dearborn, *Beyond Duty: A Passion for Christ, a Heart for Mission* (Monrovia, CA: MARC, 1998), 2; and Rowan Williams.

26. Karl Barth, *Against the Stream: Shorter Post-War Writings 1946–52* (London: SCM Press, 1954), 73.

Presiding Bishop Katharine Jefferts Schori said in 2011 that the church faces a "life-or-death decision," describing life as "a renewed and continually renewing focus on mission" and death as "an appeal to old ways and to internal focus" that devotes ever-greater resources to the institution and its internal conflict.[27] You can sense the urgency of her words. She is not alone in her concern. More and more voices across traditions and denominations are joining the quest to rediscover the church's future in the power and rigor of its past.

The prophetic insight of Loren Mead,[28] founder of the Alban Institute in the 1970s, is taking hold more firmly in the early years of the twenty-first century. Through the Institute's studies of congregational life, Mead began to note this cataclysmic shift in the way the institutional church in North America lives in the world. He asserts that the church is moving to the margins of culture and society as funding and the number of its adherents both plummet. Our governmental structures and polity were created in and reflect the monarchical era of national governments (the third to twentieth centuries CE are called the Christendom era; in America, evolving business organizational/development models influenced us further.

When Mead compares today's context with other eras, he affirms that our age is most like the first centuries of the church, known as the Apostolic Era. (Our words *apostle* and *apostolic* derive from the Greek and mean "one who is sent," or "being sent with a purpose or commission.") Thus, it is fair to say that we are in a New Apostolic Era, though this age goes by several descriptive names that add nuance and texture: postmodern, or post-Christendom, or post-Constantinian. *New Apostolic Era* is preferred in this book since it uses the more positive "new" rather than "post." *New Apostolic* also references the truth to which Mead pointed in his study.

One of the first intentional missional voices in this New Apostolic Era was that of Lesslie Newbigin, bishop in the Church of South India. He wrote:

Once again it has to be said that there can be no going back to the "Constantinian" era. It will only be by movements that begin with the local congregation in which the reality of the new creation is present, known, and experienced, and from which men and women will go into every sector of public life to claim it for Christ, to unmask the illusions which have remained hidden and to expose all areas of public life to the illumination of the gospel. But that will only happen as and when local congregations renounce an introverted concern for their own life,

---

27. Mary Frances Schjonberg, "Presiding Bishop Warns Executive Council of 'Suicide by Governance,'" Episcopal News Service (Oct. 24, 2010).

28. The prologue of this book gives a substantial introduction to the three eras that Loren Mead describes.

and recognize that they exist for the sake of those who are not members, as sign, instrument, and foretaste of God's redeeming grace for the whole life of society.[29]

If you like excitement and challenge, now is a great time to live as the church reroots itself in the Great Commission of being sent into the world. It's important to note here that we are not referring to "sending missionaries to foreign lands."[30] We are *all* missionaries wherever we go, wherever we live, whatever we do, whoever we are.

The foundation of leadership for vestry members and other parish leaders is our baptismal charge to be engaged in God's mission in the world and to point the congregation to the mission of Christ the Servant who "came not to be served but to serve" (Matt. 20:28). This is the essential "ordination" that every follower of Jesus shares. Hierarchical structures that vested authority in professional clergy are flattening as those who have additional "ordinations" resume the early church's understanding that those who are set apart as deacons, priests, or bishops are in the church not to be *above* anyone but to be *among* the people of God as equippers, enablers, mentors, and supporters of the ministry of all the baptized.

The transition to post-Christendom is marked by a movement:

From the center to margins: in Christendom the Christian story and the churches were central, but in post-Christendom narrative is marginal.

From majority to minority: Christians were the (often overwhelming) majority in Christendom, but in post-Christendom we already are or are becoming a minority.

From settlers to sojourners: in Christendom we were comfortable in a culture shaped by our story, but in post-Christendom we are aliens, exiles, and pilgrims in a culture where we no longer experience affinity.

From privilege to plurality: Christians enjoyed many privileges in Christendom, but in post-Christendom we are one community among many in a pluralistic society.

From control to witness: in Christendom churches could exert influence over society, but in post-Christendom we exercise influence only through witnessing to our story and its implications.

From maintenance to mission: in Christendom the emphasis was on maintaining a Christian status quo, but in post-Christendom, mission is within a contested environment.

From institution to movement: churches operated mainly in institutional mode in Christendom, but in post-Christendom we are again becoming a Christian movement.

---

29. Lesslie Newbigin, *The Gospel in a Pluralist Society* (Grand Rapids: Eerdmans, 1989), 232–33.

30. This should not be interpreted as disparaging the sending of missionaries to other cultures and nations.

English colonists brought to America a congregational governance structure known as vestries. They were adapted to their American context and were generally charged with governmental, institutional tasks.[31] Every person who serves on a vestry today has the opportunity to reinvent and amplify the renewed ministry of a vestry. "New occasions teach new duties,"[32] we sing. Leadership is needed now more than ever as every baptized person renews his or her claim as both a *disciple* (learner, follower) and *apostle* (person sent with a commission).

What is ahead for leaders in the near future? Let's begin with a simple definition of mission. The catechism in the Book of Common Prayer puts it this way: "The mission of the Church is to restore all people to unity with God and each other in Christ" (855). A missional church, which acknowledges and participates in God's mission, will see the signs of unity with God and each other not only within the ecclesial fellowship but also in the community where members of the congregation dwell. God is already at work in those places. The church, as the people of God who answer the call to "restore all people to unity," is seeking to join God in what is already underway.

What does this shift look like in the life of a congregation? There are three big transitions the local congregation as a missional community needs to address as they move out of a place of privilege in the old Christendom model of church and into the New Apostolic Era. Reggie McNeal describes these three transitions in *Missional Renaissance*.[33]

The first transition is *moving away from an internal focus toward an external focus*. This shift is marked by:

• deep community engagement

• moving *beyond* doing service projects or charitable acts

• mission not as an *activity* but as a way of *being* church in the world

• asking how are we seeking the reign of God

This move from an internal focus to an external focus of ministry is what most people think of when they think of a missional church. In this shift the church breaks out of its bondage to a membership culture that is fed by meeting the needs of its members. As it begins to shift the focus outward, the

---

31. In colonial Virginia, as an example of an expanded use of vestries, they were part of the actual secular governmental structure, serving as the equivalent of a town council.

32. James R. Lowell's hymn, "Once to Every Man and Nation," *The Hymnal 1940* (New York: Church Humnal, 1961), hymn 579.

33. Reggie McNeal, *Missional Renaissance: Changing the Scorecard for the Church* (San Francisco: Jossey-Bass, 2009). These shifts and their implications are explored throughout his book.

missional way may mistakenly be taken to mean an increasing involvement in community engagement events for a day of service. As well, they may see missional engagement as merely a set of activities rather than a way of being church in God's world. In this move there is nothing less than a re-visioning of the church. This shift raises the core question of why the church exists: Is it primarily to maintain the institutional forms and structures, or to be an instrument in God's hand for the extension of the reign of God?

Reggie McNeal writes, "Unfortunately, many church leaders think that simply their engagement in some kind of community service makes them missional. But this is not the case. That would reduce what it means to be missional to just another program or methodological approach to 'doing church.' . . . Moving to an external focus pushes the church from doing missions as some second-mile project into being on mission as a way of life."[34]

The second transition is *from being program-driven to the development of God's people as disciples in the world*. Elements of this shift are:

- moving away from the Christendom experience of church as a collection of programs
- realizing that viewing the church's "product" as its programmatic output creates "consumers" rather than disciples and apostles
- equipping followers of Jesus who enjoy the abundant life and point others to it
- shifting focus away from mere participation in the program life of the church toward maturation as disciples who confidently discern God's movement in the world and join it

It is common to think of churches as a collection of the programs developed to attract members. This late-twentieth-century perspective really unveils the consumerism of our culture. The question raised here is what product are we producing? The answer was to create programs, observed and encouraged (not intentionally) by Arlin Routhage through his church-size theory of becoming a "program church."[35] The assembling of a critical mass of people to provide programming meant that the congregation was no longer small (which was deemed undesirable or limiting) and had arrived at the place where, from an institutional point of view, the congregation was more real, true, or viable.

---

34. McNeal, *Missional Renaissance*, 42.

35. Dr. Routhage did helpful and pioneering work in size theory and church development and redevelopment. My critique concerns an unintended consequence. Routhage's designation of a "program size church" became a gauge that would provide validation for effective Christendom-style church by engaging a proliferation of programming.

Alternatively, the missional church is concerned with making disciples, producing followers of Jesus who are enjoying the abundant life Jesus promised and pointing others to it.

Everyday living is where we work out our salvation (see Phil. 2:12). The program-driven church may have created an artificial environment divorced from the actual rhythms and realities of normal life. The movement experienced in this second shift is from mere participation in church activities to maturation as a child of God who participates in all domains of culture as God's sons and daughters.

The third major transition is *from church-based leadership to leadership that works to continue discerning and participating in the reign of God*. Here are some of the components:

- Church-based leadership is oriented to maintenance and status quo.
- Church-based leadership is institutional, controlling, and clergy-centric.
- Missional (reign of God) leadership is empowering, organic, and reproductive.
- Missional leadership is oriented toward the community where God is already present.

The older leadership form (church-based) is a creation of the church as an institution. It is usually expressed under the roof of the church and as a church activity. When leadership is focused on the reign of God (God's desire to restore all to unity with God and each other), it moves into the world and is deployed across the full range of culture. Church-based questions include "What is our scorecard on raising the budget and attracting new members?" and "What will we celebrate among ourselves?" Missional leaders ask questions like "How are people doing?" or "Where is God at work in our community and how do we join in?" Reggie Mc-Neal again writes, "The way to shift leadership results is to change what leaders are doing and thinking about. Leaders have to live the change they seek. This is not easy; it requires ruthless self-management."[36]

The times are complex and shifting. This chapter is a glimpse of the lay of the land in this New Apostolic Era. It is only a glimpse. Please continue to study and learn. It is also true that we are somewhere in the midst of this shift and do not have a complete assessment of

> Lord God, you call your servants to ventures of which we cannot see the ending, by paths as yet untrodden, through perils unknown; give us faith to go out with good courage, not knowing where we go, but only that your hand is leading us, and your love supporting us; to the glory of your name. Amen.
>
> —Diocese of Southwell and Nottingham

---

36. McNeal, *Missional Renaissance*, 153.

the nature of these times. Continue to exercise discernment so that the local congregation, in the midst of this reformation, forms the hands and feet of Jesus in and for the world. While the shape of the times may not be fully revealed, the confidence we have is that the Holy Spirit is continuing to clothe us with "power from on high" (Luke 24:49).

RESOURCES

Read "The Five Marks of Mission" (p. 104). Our mother church, the Church of England, experienced significant attendance decline in the twentieth century. This urgency made them face the new realities and work toward rebirth. One of the guides for their renewal (later adopted across the Anglican Communion) was affirming the Five Marks of Mission. A discussion of this paper is recommended for vestries and adult study groups.

If this chapter on mission captures your attention and imagination, please read Reggie McNeal's book *Missional Renaissance* in its entirety. In the download section (p. 23) you will find access to a study guide for the book. It is an invaluable resource for any leadership group.

There is a brief theological essay on the trinitarian foundation of mission in part two, entitled "The Story We Tell and the Story God Tells" (see p. 107).

DISCUSSION

How have you experienced the shift that is being named: the move from Christendom to post-Christendom?

What changes have occurred in your faith community that seem to result from this shift? What changes in attendance? In funding? In participation? In securing leaders?

Where is your congregation in its navigation of the three transitions:
from an internal to an external focus?
from program driven to disciple development?
from institutional, church-based leadership to leaders focused on participating in the reign of God?

CHAPTER 7
Principled Practices by Keeping
COVENANT

Jeremiah the prophet put it this way: "I will be your God, and you shall be my people; and walk only in the way I command you, so that it may be well with you" (Jer. 7:23). The concept of covenant reaches back to the founding story of our forebears in faith. Covenant agreements between God and the people of God are a hallmark of how we organize relationships.

God's covenant with our forebears also reroots the church as the people of God with mission as their primary purpose. In Genesis, this covenant is given: "Now the Lord said to Abram, 'Go from your country and your kindred and your father's house to the land that I will show you. I will make of you a great nation and I will bless you, and make your name great, so that you will be a blessing. I will bless those who bless you, and the one who curses you I will curse; and in you all the families of the earth will be blessed'" (Gen. 12:1–3). Note well the directionality of God granting blessing to Abraham and Sarah and their descendants. Essentially, God is saying, "You will be blessed so that you will be a blessing to everyone else." God says, "All the people of the earth will be blessed through you." The shift for a missional church is away from an internal focus toward a greater concern for those who are outside the faith community. The intention is that the faithful are a blessing in the community *because they have been blessed by God*. The purpose of covenant is to accept and extend blessing.

The establishment of a Vestry Covenant (or a Youth Covenant, an Outreach Team Covenant, or a Choir Covenant) is a way to move toward a healthy, principled future for your church and its operation as part of the body of Christ. The shape of the blessing you will offer to the place where God has set you as a community of faith will be as unique as the geography around you. A covenant clears away the confusion and sets a simple, biblical model for life together.

Here is an example of a Vestry Covenant:

> We are a people of *abundance* and *grace*. We express this commitment by making our conversations and actions holy and life affirming. We work hard to remove deficit-based words and expressions from our speech. As people of light, we believe in direct communication and do not participate in communication triangles (speaking of others who are not present); we believe that anonymous information (folks not willing to be quoted) has no place in our life together. We are a permission-giving people who will strive to say "yes" to each other and God by recognizing the bounty God has given us. Our purpose is Godly, prayerful, open, engaging, consensus-seeking discernment of God's mission for our congregation in the world. God blesses us so that we may be a blessing in our community.

Within this example are several elements that one vestry determined to be healthy practice. There is the principle of abundance and the reduction of deficit-based language. In this model there are two practices that will be given particular attention in this chapter: direct communication and anonymous information. Attention to both is recommended for inclusion in every covenant.

On a body such as a vestry there will be differences of opinion. In the wider parish family there will be differences of opinion. It cannot be stressed enough that for one's own soul's health and for the upbuilding of the body of Christ, the only proper way to deal with issues that divide is by speaking directly and openly with the person or persons with whom one disagrees.

It is a human trait to fear this direct communication. Consequently, people often speak behind the backs of those with whom they have disagreement. Such indirect communication, called *communication triangles* (and sometimes called *gossip*, *backbiting*, or *sabotage*), is unseemly within the church. Yet, to be honest, we must expect it since the metaphor often used to describe the local church is that of family–the very place where we learn our basic (and sometimes unhealthy) communication patterns. Persons who are in crisis often work out their problems through the church family. Leaders have a special responsibility to set a high moral tone and not allow themselves to become embroiled in indirect communication. It is always best to point persons who have disagreements with another person directly to that person. Being the third party in a discussion is rarely constructive. It is truly a ministry of healing to urge persons with such "baggage" to go directly to those who trouble them.

> For lack of wood the fire goes out, and where there is no whisperer, quarreling ceases.
>
> —Proverbs 26:20

As pertains to meetings of the vestry or any leadership group, direct communication means the full expression of one's thoughts and feelings at meetings and not later disparaging the work of the vestry or group outside the confines of the meeting room. This latter type of behavior manifests itself in parking-lot discussions, telephone calls, or poison e-mails. Communication triangles may also be seen in people who try to build alliances outside of normal, healthy channels in order to bolster their opinion or position on a matter. Full participation in open, honest, and graced discussion will mean that such *sub rosa* methods are never necessary. Such healthy, open communication benefits the body of Christ.

Another healthy operating principle has further implications for positive, open, above-board communication. Make it your practice never to introduce anonymous suggestions or critiques into vestry discussions (or any church discussion). These are the comments that generally run like this: "One or two people have said such and such to me." or "There are some people who do (or don't) like such and such."

Anonymous comments are *never* helpful or healthy in a godly environment. In order to introduce any comment from anyone else in a vestry discussion, the owner of the thought must be stated. If a person is not willing to have his or her name associated with the thought or suggestion, it is not worthy of consideration. The owner of an opinion is always invited to present his or her comment in person.

This approach will prove invaluable in keeping all communication clear, direct, and clean, as well as in avoiding debilitating communication triangles.

There are unique qualities in every local congregation and in all its various ministry groups. There are qualities that build the faith community and attributes that deter or diminish the making of disciples. Lifting up those qualities that seek the movement of the Holy Spirit expressed in the form of a covenant is both formative and sustaining. Covenanting together affirms the attributes of a particular people in a particular place in service toward the unique purpose of God for that place and serves to support a cultural change for people to be credible missionaries.

RESOURCES

In the resource section see especially "A Primer on Permission-Giving Churches" (p. 112). This practice is contained in the example covenant and helps overcome the human reticence to try new things and new ways.

See also "Creating a Vestry Covenant" (p. 115).

DISCUSSION

Discuss with your vestry or team the elements you think would be needed in a vestry or congregational covenant. The covenant may be used as a model for other groups (choir, youth group, fellowship group) in the congregation.

What are your personal experiences with communication triangles? How did you deal with them?

Have you ever encountered or used anonymous information to insert uncomfortable or negative information into a conversation? How did it affect you and the conversation?

CHAPTER 8
Staying Grounded as
DISCIPLES

Disciple at its core means learner. In today's environment of flattened hierarchy, we are rediscovering that we are all learners—lifelong learners. Because of our need for continual renewal and refreshment, we never leave the basic posture of being a disciple of Jesus Christ. This sets loose in us the desire to align ourselves with the story of God's love engaging the world.

The context for our formation is in the community, especially in our faith community, the local congregation. Henri Nouwen wrote, "It is in community that we are tested and purified. It is in community that we learn what forgiveness and healing are all about. It is in community that we learn who our neighbor is. Community is the true school of love."[37] The primary way we learn to be disciples is by being around and in interaction with others who are disciples. The role of a leader is to help these interactions occur and to participate regularly in such interactions.

How do we do this? It is perhaps not so much a matter of our own doing as it is making space for God to act upon us, in us, and through us. One of the essential ways we make space for God is to interact with the story of who God is and who we are. Vestries (and every other leadership team) will find the strength for their mission in ongoing Bible study and prayer. While this may be a feature of parish life in other contexts, it is good that study and prayer be part of each meeting of the vestry. The shape of this study should be your own. There are several simple models that can serve

> Christianity does not consist in any partial amendment of our lives, any particular moral virtues, but in an entire change of our natural temper, a life wholly devoted to God.
>
> —William Law

---

37. Henri Nouwen in the introduction to *Discipleship: Living for Christ in the Daily Grind* by J. Heinrich Arnold (Rifton, NY: Plough Publishing House, 2011), x.

your ongoing discipleship training (see the resources section). Some of these approaches are *lectio divina*, African Bible Study, and Dwelling in the Word. The essential piece is that there be a purposeful reflection on the connection between the biblical story and the individual and collective experience of the members of the vestry.

We all recognize the presence of sin in the church, that human condition that draws us away from the love of God. The disciple dimension of life in the church is a remedy for one of the common expressions of sin known as hubris or pride. The disciple always knows that she or he is a lifelong learner and is still a work in progress under the guidance of the Holy Spirit. Another gift given by discipleship is the reminder that we are not a source of power or control; we are created, not the Creator. All baptized persons, no matter their ordination or leadership status, are equally disciples.

The disciple function goes hand-in-glove with being an apostle. Jesus's first followers were described as both disciples and apostles. When Jesus called them together, they were bound together in a learning community. Those earliest days with the Master were formative; it oriented them to their base community as a source of strength and nurture. As they grew in their knowledge and love of the Lord, Jesus began to trust them to go out to teach and heal. When the time came for Jesus to return to the Father, he pronounces a general commission—The Great Commission—that his followers should "go into all the world." The disciple is now also an apostle (a "sent person") with a mission.

Discipleship is the ongoing formation of the people of God as followers of Jesus Christ. Apostleship is the response of all the baptized to the mission of God to be missionary people whose vocation is to carry, in word and deed, the Good News into every part of the world. Apostolic leaders embody this redemptive movement into the world and by so doing call forth and authenticate the apostolic calling of all God's people.

There is in these two roles a twinned dynamism. Discipleship takes the form of a learner and apostleship takes the form of a giver. The disciple knows that she or he needs continual formation in the way of God as it is deeply explored in study, prayer, fellowship, and worship. The apostle knows that he or she has a calling to be with a God who is on the move in the world to extend the reign of God's redemption, of making whole, of binding up, of declaring Good News. Together the discipleship-apostleship dyad makes a whole: a place to take in nourishment and refreshment (discipleship) paired with a place to go to serve in mission to a world through one's life and witness in every venue of life. This dyad is transformed into a triad as it participates in God's continuing presence that we call the Holy Spirit. Especially in our Anglican context this presence is mediated through worship where "we unite ourselves with others to acknowledge the holiness of God, to hear God's Word, to offer prayer, and to celebrate the sacraments."[38]

Perhaps the best interplay of discipleship and apostleship is that they provide a natural action-reflection model for our growth as missionaries. The interplay of the people of God as they oscillate between apostleship and discipleship creates a vibrant community of Christian practice with strong, mutual companionship and conversation. This oscillation is the core experience that keeps in balance the life inside the church with its divine mission outside the church. The leader calls attention to "the particular community, empowered by God's Spirit, (which) not only lives out the gospel internally but opens up the gospel externally by the way it lives, so that others may see and respond."[39]

> We cannot worship Jesus at the altar if we do not serve him in the streets.
> —Bishop Frank Weston

RESOURCES

There are sample guides for Bible study on p. 117 of the resource section.

There is a primer on the action-reflection model on p. 122 of the resource section.

If oscillation theory interests you, see Bruce Reed, *The Dynamics of Religion: Process and Movement in Christian Churches* (London: Darton, Longman and Todd, 1978).

DISCUSSION

What transformative impact does attentiveness to discipleship formation have (or potentially have) in your congregation?

Do you currently have a time for Bible study and reflection as part of your vestry meeting? If so, what disciple-building function does it provide? If not, what might be added to a vestry meeting through a Bible study method?

What is the link, in your assessment, between being formed as a disciple and being sent into the world?

---

38. The Catechism in the Book of Common Prayer (New York: Chruch Publishing, 1979), 857.

39. Darrell L. Guder, ed., *Missional Church: A Vision for the Sending of the Church in North America* (Grand Rapids: Eerdmans, 1998), 247.

CHAPTER 9

Growth Is
Grounded in Positive
CHANGE

In 1914, Thomas Edison's laboratory was virtually destroyed by fire. The damage exceeded two million dollars and was insured for only a tenth of that amount since the buildings were made of concrete and thought to be fireproof. Much of Edison's life's work went up in flames. At the height of the fire, Edison's son frantically sought out his father amid the smoke and debris. He finally found him calmly watching the conflagration. Edison was contemplative and reflective.

Edison's son said he ached for him; everything was gone. When Edison saw his son, he asked after his wife and said, "Where's your mother? Find her. Bring her here. She will never see anything like this as long as she lives." The following morning, Edison looked at the ruins of what had been his laboratory and said, "There is great value in disaster. All our mistakes are burned up. Thank God we can start anew." Three weeks after the fire, Edison managed to deliver his first phonograph.[40]

Fire also has significant meaning for the church's genesis. Remember Pentecost: "When the day of Pentecost had come, they were all together in one place. And suddenly from heaven there came a sound like the rush of a violent wind, and it filled the entire house where they were sitting. Divided tongues, as of fire, appeared among them, and a tongue rested on each of them. All of them were filled with the Holy Spirit and began to speak in other languages, as the Spirit gave them ability" (Acts 2:1–4).

---

40. Michael Hansbury, *The Quality of Leadership* (New Delhi: Epitome Books, 2009), 40.

Dramatic change became the substance out of which was born a great discovery. In Edison's case, old ideas and mistakes were carried away and the way was prepared for fresh, creative thinking. In the case of the early church, the once-fearful band experienced new energy for participation in mission marked by "signs and wonders," generosity, and remarkable growth in number of followers in the Way. The Holy Spirit, the abiding presence of God, is sent to lead the church in its participation in the reign of God.

The fire of Pentecost and the sending of the Spirit

> created the Church, the community of Jesus Christ. The Holy Spirit lifted up the community into the very life of God: Father, Son, and Holy Spirit. The Spirit empowered the community to pray [to the Father] as free, adopted, children of God. . . . [T]he community is empowered to go forth to proclaim the Good News of God to all peoples and nations. The Holy Spirit is the unifying force of God in the community. The unity of the Church which is given, and yet which it seeks to deepen, is grounded in the very unity of God.[41]

The Greek word *metanoia* contains a basic premise of Scripture and our spiritual development. Consider this, from the gospel of Mark: "The time is fulfilled, and the kingdom of God has come near; repent (*metanoia*), and believe in the good news" (Mark 1:15). In English this "turn," "change of mind," or "invitation to go beyond our present outlook" is often translated "repent." Jesus, therefore, believes that change is normal and necessary in the Christian life. Our human experience teaches us that change is not optional. Change is simply part of the human condition. What Jesus wishes us to harness is purposeful change that points us to and helps us experience the Good News.

Change, however, is not necessarily easy. We all resist change, some of us more than others. Consider this variance in change adaptability as simply one more piece of diversity in any leadership group. It is not normally a case of some being good and others of us being not-so-good or bad.

Since stagnation is not the goal of any congregation, leaders will always be dealing with the reality of change. An effective way to move toward any change is to promise that the best of what has been or is will always be carried forward.[42] In one congregation there was a devotion to the early days of the founding of the church. There had been much hands-on work by the members. As the church grew and grew, there were opportunities to simply

---

41. Virginia Report, *The Inter-Anglican Theological and Doctrinal Commission (Secretary General of the Anglican Consultative Council,* 1997), 12.

42. The promise to carry forward is not that some specific thing or action will be locked in place, but rather that the principle or vision *standing behind* that honored piece of history will be preserved.

purchase new turnkey buildings. However, to honor those who remembered what they referred to as the "pioneer days," something was always left professionally unfinished so that members could do the work. Older members got to use their hands and newer members got to have a taste of the pioneer days. The best of what was is carried forward and those who might have resisted change are honored by having that which they cherish brought forward.

There is, however, another approach to change that lives and moves among us. Thus far change has been presented from an appreciative approach, but there is another reality possible within change, and that possibility is conflict.

> Everybody has accepted by now that change is unavoidable. But that still implies that change is like death and taxes—it should be postponed as long as possible and no change would be vastly preferable. But in a period of upheaval, such as the one we are living in, change is the norm.
>
> —Peter Drucker

When possible, it is best to reframe conflict into opportunities. Sometimes this reframing is not possible and conflict moves in unhealthy and toxic directions. The key point here is that unless leaders are skilled in conflict management, substantive conflict requires outside facilitation. Your diocesan office is your resource for assistance here.[43]

The point of chapter 2, "Cultivating Health through Modeling," is to underscore the need for the creation of an appreciative (nondeficit) atmosphere in the congregation. Appreciative Inquiry also offers tools for implementing discernment for mission and ministry. The appreciative approach uses positive, strategic questions with the people of God gathered in your congregation. As this wisdom is gathered, patterns evolve that move the group through Appreciative Inquiry's 4-D Cycle. Here it is in outline:

Discover: Seek to understand the "best of what is" and "what has been." Craft appreciative interview questions that seek the "positive core." These questions usually generate stories to enrich the images and inner dialogue within the organization and to bring the positive core more fully into focus. This inspires the emergence of organic, maybe unanticipated, changes well before implementation of the more purposeful phases of the 4-D Cycle.

Dream: This phase is an energizing exploration of "what might be," a time for people to explore their hopes and dreams for their church and its place in the world at large. It is a time for groups of people to engage in thinking big, thinking out of the box, and thinking out of the historical boundaries (the congregation's past). The Dream phase seeks to identify and spread generative, affirmative, and hopeful images of the future. Typically, this is accomplished in large-group forums, where combinations of parishioners explore

---

43. See "Navigating Church Conflict" (p. 125).

creative images, innovative strategic visions, and an elevated sense of purpose.

Design: Choices are now made about "what should be" within the church. It is a conscious re-creation or transformation, through which such things as systems, structures, strategies, processes, and images will become more fully aligned with the church's *positive past* (Discover) and its *highest potential* (Dream).

Deliver: This phase seeks a series of inspired actions that support ongoing learning and innovation or "what will be." Since the entire 4-D Cycle provides an open forum for everyone to contribute and step forward in the service of the church, change occurs in all phases of an Appreciative Inquiry process. The Deliver phase, however, focuses specifically on personal and congregational commitments and paths forward. The result is generally an extensive array of changes throughout the church.

In most cases, the 4-D Cycle provides the framework for *ongoing* activities. Thus, the cycle begins again . . . and again . . . and again. *The greatest payoff for using Appreciative Inquiry is shifting congregational culture away from problem solving and deficit mindedness toward a more hopeful, abundant culture.* Leadership in congregations that have discovered their appreciative energy move from chore to joy. What is established is a culture of naming and expecting the best the people of God have to offer. Leaders both help build this culture and tap it to facilitate positive change in the congregation as it lives into God's mission.

❧

Paul Chaffee[44] held a part-time interim pastorate in a small congregation in a rural area that was labeled by some as in its death throes and therefore deserving a dignified funeral. "Instead it bounced back and is thriving today," Chaffee wrote. "During an 18-month interim I approached the prayers of the people in a new way. Following the Sunday sermon, I took paper and pen and walked into the middle of the congregation, barely a dozen those first few months. I invited them to reflect on the past week and share things they were thankful for and things that concerned them. People poured out their hearts. Following what were sometimes 15-minute discussions, I would lead them in prayer, mentioning all the thanksgivings, all the petitions, and together we concluded with the Lord's Prayer."

Chaffee concludes: "A year later the coffee-hour conversations were all

---

44. Paul Chaffee wrote chapter 4 in *www.congregationalresources.org: A Guide to Congregational Resources for Building Congregational Vitality*, ed. Richard Bass (Herndon, VA: Alban Institute, 2004), 67–99. The other chapters and their topics also are worth a read.

about answered prayer. It didn't dawn on me until three years later, after taking an Appreciative Inquiry intensive, that we had developed an appreciative approach to the prayers of the people in that small church. We heard each other talk about what was important enough to be thankful for and important enough to share with God as a concern. As the year progressed, the subject of answered prayers came up again and again, to continued thanks."[45]

Life returned to a "dying" church. Similar explorations await every aspect of congregational life.

RESOURCES

There is a large online collection of resources for the study and use of Appreciative Inquiry. These resources pertain to a broad spectrum of organizations and institutions, some specifically focused upon the church. The recommended starting place is the Appreciative Inquiry Commons website at http://appreciativeinquiry.case.edu/. Appreciative Inquiry is an open source process. See also the Appreciative Inquiry Primer on page 93 of the resource section in this book.

Conflict is found wherever human beings gather. The church is no exception. See the discussion of this reality in Navigating Church Conflict on page 125 of the resource section.

DISCUSSION

What is the history of change in your congregation? What worked? What were the challenges?

Like Edison, if all your church's mistakes burned up, what would remain? For what would the removal of mistakes make room?

What objectives do you have that might benefit from a 4-D process?

---

45. Chaffee, *www.congregationalresources.org,* 89.

CHAPTER 10

Vestry as a Seedbed for
LEADERSHIP

There is a seismic shift underway in the church as we move away from the old Christendom era in which the church held a privileged place. Today, in this New Apostolic Era, the church (as the people of God) is moving to the margins of society with a new (perhaps *re*newed) commitment to God's mission. A leader is a person who is aware of the change and committed to work in this new context.[46]

> Leadership is a process by which a person influences others gracefully and honorably to accomplish God's purposes and together direct the church in a way that is faithful in its pursuit of mission.

Where do leaders come from who have the ability to discern the times and guide the church—the people of God—as it finds the place, shape, and mission God has prepared for it in a changed and changing world? To give the church its necessary leadership, the vestry might be thought of as a school for leadership development. Every congregation has a vestry. With a re-purposing of some of the time spent together, space can be created for formation. Healthy, proliferative leaders, given the three-year rotation on vestries, "graduate" annually and continue giving their gifts in the faith community.

What is it that they take with them? The most important keys to godly leadership are being trustworthy and visionary.[47] While pointed out in secular studies of leadership, both of these elements are grounded in the sacramental

---

46. While this discussion focuses upon leadership as a process of positive relational influence, it must be noted that there will be those who exercise relational influence that is unhelpful, obstructionist, or negative. Please see "Navigating Church Conflict" (p. 125) in the resource section if this is part of your congregation's life together.

47. These are explored in Larry F. Lamb and Kathy Brittain McKee, *Applied Public Relations: Cases in Stakeholder Management* (Mahwah, NJ: Lawrence Erlbaum Associates, 2004).

character[48] of the church. The inner coherence of a leader is established in trustworthiness; the outward character of leadership is seen as the leader shows a way forward that is faithful and visionary.

Every leader is unique and will offer a range of some of the principles and skills described in this book to encourage the church forward. Those who serve as members of the vestry will find opportunities for the intentional building of leadership skills. Over time, healthy, generative, useful patterns of enacting the mission of the church crowd out any elements of church life that would derail honoring the Great Commission of Jesus (Matt. 28:16–20)[49] and the Great Commandment (Matt. 22:34–40).[50] These commitments will likely be summarized in the church's covenant.

The discussion thus far has addressed leadership in a community context. Leaders together utilize these capacities to serve the mission and ministry of the church. This concluding chapter looks at six disciplines or competencies of personal leadership that help leaders develop trust and vision. Those who serve on the vestry are invited to tend to the development of these competencies for transformative leadership. God does prepare all of us to serve in each of these ways, but it is our task to train ourselves for their best use in the councils of the church and in shifting our church's culture toward a more positive, missional, life-giving reality.

The Focus Competency

The gift and discipline of focus enhances the ability to see rightly. In this New Apostolic Era, the leader who can focus offers insight, correction, and over-the-horizon vision. The leader who practices the discipline of focus serves as an example and encourages the people to refocus regularly for course correction, seeing new opportunities and refinement of mission. Focused leaders carry the gift of vision. In fact, offering the skill of focus can be the difference in moving forward or being stymied.

Any competency you choose to access is a combination of skill and talent that may be developed for your own personal edification and for the good of the community. The ability to focus is essential in any development of skills and talents. Like a magnifying glass set to the sun, focus is the means by which it becomes possible to concentrate the diffuse rays of our thoughts and actions

---

48. The Prayer Book defines a sacrament as "an outward and visible sign of an inward and spiritual grace." The Book of Common Prayer (New York: Church Publishing, 1979), 857.

49. See also Mark 16:14–18, Luke 24:44–49, Acts 1:4–8, and John 20:19–23. These passages, and those following, would form a compelling Bible study for a vestry.

50. See also Mark 12:28–34 and Luke 10:25–28.

into a sharp point of light. This bright light of focus becomes a guiding light like the pillar of fire given the people of Israel to guide them in their journey (Exod. 13, 14).

The Relational Competency

Our relationships and the quality of those relationships are a good measure of the work of the Holy Spirit in our lives. We tend our relationships because God is revealed to us as a relational God in the Holy Trinity. The quality of human relationships is marked by the building of communities of reconciliation and renewal that create the experience of forgiveness, justice, hope, healing, and grace in and beyond our community of faith. Our leadership begins in and is sustained through our relationship with Christ.

The primary reason for leadership failure is the inability to build relationships and a team environment, says a recent global study. From the positive side, when naming factors that contribute to success, more relational abilities topped the list: fitting oneself in the organization's values and culture, interpersonal skills, motivation to lead, and experience. "What emerges from the survey analysis is that leadership success is increasingly dependent on getting along with others in the organization as well as with one's own team. A leader must be able to connect, build relationships, and be flexible enough to adapt to the . . . culture."[51]

Leaders who develop their relationship competency will help the church of the twenty-first century thrive.

The Servant Competency

"I am among you as one who serves," said Jesus (Luke 22:27b). Of particular note is that Jesus says this just after he rebukes the disciples, reminding them that leadership does not derive from having power over people. One of the markers of the change we are experiencing in this shift from the Christendom experience is the flattening of hierarchy. To the degree that leaders have patterned their leadership style after the old command-and-control approach, competency in this new age will necessitate a return to an old, biblical way: servant leadership.

> One thing I know: the only ones among you who will be really happy are those who will have sought and found how to serve.
>
> —Albert Schweitzer

The servant leader is one who moves out of the descriptions of one's place in the leadership hierarchy and

---

51. "Poor Relationships Top Cause for Leadership Failure," Right Management news release (Nov. 15, 2011), www.right.com.

into a concern for the deep well-being and growth in grace of her or his fellow travelers. Competency in servant leadership grows out of a motivation that genuinely serves the good of the church. There is no particular demeanor required; gregarious, shy, simple, energetic, humble, and confident people all qualify. The essential characteristic is motivation. The servant leader unleashes the gifts of those whom he or she leads and benefits the mission of the church.

In this age of the significant shifting and reformation in culture and the church, the role of the servant leader is growing in importance. To develop this competency means that the people of God have a hopeful companion in the midst of change. Anxiety in the community is normal as change unfolds. A grounded servant-leader contributes confidence that change need not be destructive, but is rather a way forward.[52]

The Navigational Competency

In turbulent times the ability to navigate helps the church (the people of God) find a way forward, especially when they feel stuck. Navigators are concerned with the topography of our world. As such, they are particularly adept at reading the environment and ensuring good processes while traversing known and unknown territory. The navigational competency is vital to a church charting a course from old, tired, and lifeless ways to newer, vital, missional ways of being God's church.

Specifically, the navigator pays attention to position, has skills at planning the journey, advises other leaders on timing and destinations, and warns of hazards along the way. What navigators do is to focus their competence in areas of strategic importance for the sake of those who travel with them.

> If you want to build a ship, then don't drum up people to gather wood, give orders, and divide the work. Rather, teach them to yearn for the far and endless sea.
>
> —Antoine de Saint-Exupery

In any faith community experiencing stress, loss, or fear of the old ways disappearing, a navigator serves the church by helping to make sense of the "between times," the time when Christendom is fading and that which is coming to be is not yet here. Navigators point us in the right direction.

Jesus is a navigator in the story of walking on water (Matt. 14:22–33). The disciples, in a boat, are battered by the elements and afraid they might drown. Jesus, walking on the water, comes to them and says, "Take heart . . . do not be

---

52. There is a growing body of literature that discusses servant leadership. The first to openly reflect on this leadership style is Robert K. Greenleaf, *The Servant as Leader* (Westfield, IN: Robert K. Greenleaf Center, 1991). It is recommended to those who would like to go deeper. See also "Introduction to Servant Leadership" (p. 130) in part two of this book.

afraid" (v. 27). And when Peter, a navigator-in-training, fails at his attempt to walk on water, the experienced Navigator guides him back to safety. For Peter, it is another learning experience.

The navigational competency has as its gift the provision of safe passage. Since life is a passage, the ability of leaders to navigate is essential.

The Equipping Competency

The equipping leader realizes that one of his or her most significant services is to affirm and acknowledge the ministry of all the baptized. Leaders who are equippers take their own baptismal vows seriously and see to it that provision is made in the congregation for the forming and sending of the people of God. These provisions honor the locus of mission in the world, near and far. The equipping leader never stops learning and makes it possible for others to be lifelong learners. Leaders who tend to their own spiritual development desire the same opportunity for the whole people of God.

An essential component of equipping is that the leader is able to use her or his questions as a primary tool for urging people toward their optimum capacity as ministers of the church in the world. Wise and timely questions by an equipping leader help orient people toward their own gifts and abilities to serve. Questions allow people to take personal responsibility, releasing their own graced responsibility to take upon themselves the task at hand. Further, questions move discussions out of a hierarchical culture that prevents initiative and ownership. An equipping leader who is appreciative constantly seeks ways to empower the people of God. Saint Paul, in his discussion of the call laid upon leaders, said that Jesus' intent is "to equip the saints for the work of ministry, for building up the body of Christ" (Eph. 4:12), which has the effect of creating unity and maturity in believers.

The Self-Awareness Competency

A leader who is self-aware is marked by balance, humility, and knowledge of his or her limitations and gifts. Those who possess self-awareness are rarely jerked around by their own fallenness and by being aware keep these negative dispositions out of the communal area where they may become stumbling blocks. Self-awareness allows the setting of appropriate boundaries and the release of the talent that God has given the leader. In the congregation, a self-aware leader can provide the gift of nonanxious presence. In these times of rapid change, such a gift is needful.

Following the declaration of his sonship at his baptism, Jesus' experience encountering the adversary in the wilderness (Matt. 4) is instructive. At the end of his forty-day sojourn, the tempter came to him offering power and glory. At the root of Jesus' ability to resist the temptation was self-awareness. For Jesus and us, that which releases our ability to be aware is the same: the word spoken at Jesus' baptism of being "beloved" and the word spoken over us in our baptism of being loved by God.

With a secure identity, leaders can clearly perceive the positive core out of which they respond in and through relationships. This core is constructed of thoughts and emotions, strengths and weaknesses, beliefs and motivations. The gift given to the community by the self-aware is a preview of where healthy actions and thoughts can take a local congregation. With forethought, leaders are able to make necessary changes to focus on greater possibilities in life. Self-awareness is learned by focusing attention on our behaviors and personality. Paying attention develops the people of God.

Good leadership is not really about finding the requisite number of members with the right skill set. Rather, it is more having a faithful context where effective leadership can take hold. This context will be nourished by reciprocity with a rich interaction of many skills, talents, and capacities. It is in this interaction that all are given the opportunity to stretch and grow.

We come to the end. This part of the book, as its basic intention, has sought to survey the landscape and provide a collection of tools for the cultivation of God's mission in "fields (that) are ripe for harvesting" (John 4:35). Together we have noted ten functions of the vestry that will cultivate leaders in a reimagined form of leadership in a community of faith. This list of functions is not exhaustive; for a tree to be robust it needs an intricate system of roots and nutrients. You will no doubt find other useful ways to make leadership in the church more vigorous, effective, and missional. As this new era unfolds, we will need to be nimble and ready to faithfully shape the church to keep it true to our baptismal promises to repent, proclaim Christ, seek and serve him in all persons, and strive for peace and justice among all.

There is a godly legacy left by leaders who build and nourish a church that is drawn together to serve each other and God's world. An atmosphere of health is created when people feel honored for their contributions, knowing that it is not about self-interest but about the mission of God. The people of God learn to lead from their gifts—corporately and individually—rather than from "shoulds" and "oughts." The people grow in self-awareness, maturity, and ability to honor God and serve God's people. This is my prayer for you.

"Finally, beloved, whatever is true, whatever is honorable, whatever is just, whatever is pure, whatever is pleasing, whatever is commendable, if there is any excellence and if there is anything worthy of praise, think about these things" (Phil. 4:8).

RESOURCES

On page 129 in the resource section you will find a "Competencies Self-Assessment," an exercise for use in a vestry or other meeting to name and extend these six competencies to serve the church and God's mission in the world. These six competencies are all present on your vestry or leadership team. This exercise will help you identify those who have developed competencies for immediate use on a vestry or leadership team.

Also see "Introduction to Servant Leadership" on page 130 of the resource section.

DISCUSSION

Leadership may be defined as "a process by which a person influences others gracefully and honorably to accomplish God's purposes and together direct the church in a way that is faithful." Is this compatible with your definition?

Are you particularly adept at one or more of the competencies? What or who helped you develop that skill or ability?

What is your prayer for your vestry? For your church?

Epilogue

The ideas and principles held up in this book as transformative were born in the field by practitioners of leadership—lay and ordained—in the church. There have been many laboratories where these concepts have been explored, probed, tested, and utilized. One such laboratory is the Church of the Good Shepherd in Augusta, Georgia. Good Shepherd is a church that was strong and healthy by all Christendom standards. It is large for an Episcopal church. It is well resourced in finances and buildings. There is plenty of staff, a great choir, Sunday school, fellowship groups, youth groups, adult studies, a parochial school, outreach, and more to testify to the church's stability and viability.

In 2002, the church began significant renovations and new construction. Attendance was at an all-time high. After construction was completed, the rector, the Rev. Robert Fain, said, "We had needed additional space and we built it. Now we waited for the people and for the growth that would come." Instead, attendance began to gradually decrease. For several years, leaders tried to get a grasp on what was happening.

The vestry attended the annual leadership conference at Kanuga in 2009. There they were introduced to an evaluative tool known as the Congregational Life Cycle.[53] The next year the vestry returned to the same conference and heard the Rev. Dr. Reggie McNeal. These two events began to provide an understanding of the dynamics at work in the church. The rector wrote, "The Congregational Life Cycle offered some insight to the trends at Good Shepherd but did not fully explain what was happening in our parish. It would be Dr. McNeal's presentation that convinced the Vestry that the decades-long change in a Christendom-shaped culture had come even to Augusta, Georgia, and was impacting life and ministry at Good Shepherd."[54]

---

53. See the online downloadable resource section (p. 21) for a Congregational Life Cycle guide.

54. Robert Fain, *From Place of Purpose to Peddle of Purpose* (Augusta, GA: Church of the Good Shepherd, 2011), 7.

The leaders at the church believed that clarity was evolving and that their mission was coming into focus. Their change of direction took a particular course. After determining that the church was in a declining phase, as deduced through the Congregational Life Cycle, leaders set off on a course to learn of the changes circling round them (and all churches). The Christendom realities were fading and the contextual shifts described by Loren Mead and others bore down on their church. The vestry did the initial work of analyzing its life through the Life Cycle tool. Through its use they determined that Good Shepherd Church was experiencing diminished energy. The vestry also studied the paradigm shift signaling the movement from Christendom toward post-Christendom.[55] The leaders shared their initial work with the congregation and then began a series of discernment events for the whole parish. Their principle was that the more people connected to the mission and life of the church, the more they would "own" God's purpose and calling through the church. In the eighteen-month process that was engaged, the church employed most of the principles and concepts in this book.

The first event for the people of the church was based on the truth of Appreciative Inquiry: seek the best. All were asked to "tell of an experience in the Church of the Good Shepherd where you felt closest to God." The rector reflected on the experience. "This exercise, which was called 'Thin Places,' attested that the Body of Christ in this place is built of the living stones who share this time and their lives with each other. Together, we are a living sacrament set forth to share God's love and grace made known to us in the most amazing sacrament of all—Jesus Christ our Lord."[56] Getting in touch with the abundance of God present in and through the people of the church was encouraging and energizing. Another benefit experienced was that resistance to change was substantially diminished when the best of what is lays the foundation from which the new may grow.

After tapping into God's goodness, the congregation turned their focus to the place where God had planted them 142 years earlier. Using the information available to every Episcopal Church at www.episcopalchurch.org under "Studying Your Congregation,"[57] the congregation sought to learn who was their neighbor. If God is a God of mission, an old truth into which the church was rerooting, then they needed to know the needs and circumstances of the

---

55. This process was facilitated by consultants.

56. Fain, *From Place of Purpose*, 10.

57. The information the church used was provided by *Percept*. Similar information is now available through *MissionInsite*. The Episcopal Church has a contract with MissionInsite for demographic data. Some dioceses have contracts with these organizations. Both companies offer their tailored services (for a fee) to any church. The demographic information on the Episcopal Church website is free.

people around them. Gathered around tables in their parish hall, they looked at the demographic information and asked what issues the church might address on behalf of the community. They reminded themselves that any church named for the Good Shepherd must follow the example of their Lord and seek out those who struggle with any experience of being lost.

The third all-parish event was an evening of great fun and activity as the congregation used Asset Mapping[58] to uncover the richness present in and among the people. Using the process described in chapter 3 and in the "Introduction to Asset-Based Ministry" on page 98 in the resource section of this book, the people of Good Shepherd posted 1,500 gifts, blessings, talents, and assets on the walls of their parish hall. "One could feel the energy rise in the room as those seated at tables engaged each other in conversation, light bulbs going off in people's minds one after the other, as it became clearer and clearer to them the gifts that they and others at the table had to give to God," said Robert Fain. Asset mapping moved the Church of the Good Shepherd from "How do we get people to do things which help the church?" to "How can we possibly use all these gifts God is giving for the glory of God and for the welfare of God's people?"

The next time the congregation gathered for one of their all-parish events they saw a video called *Everyday Creativity*.[59] Fr. Fain reflects, "The awareness generated by this video is that our individual and collective perspectives form a lens which either constricts or expands our point of view. A widened point of view can unleash creativity and energy. In the church, the story of Jesus is a constant invitation to see things as God sees them. Tending to our perspectives helps us open ourselves to see and participate in God's redemptive mission in the world, a process nurtured in the church and then carried into the neighborhood, the community and the world."[60]

The last gathering in this discovery process had as a centerpiece a presentation by a priest associate of the church, the Reverend Ginny Inman. The fifth gathering was both a celebration and a charge. Inman said,

> Next to the Blessed Sacrament itself, your neighbor is the holiest object presented to your senses.
>
> —C. S. Lewis

---

58. This process was used in place of the typical approach in stewardship season pledge drives: the Time and Talent Survey. These surveys probe the congregation to fill pre-existing needs in the congregation. Asset Mapping is far more open-ended, with work plans being made based on the assets being offered. Further, so many gifts of time and talent go underutilized that many feel that it is a purposeless exercise. A commitment the leaders made in asset mapping was that at least one gift is used from every giver within six months.

59. Everyday Creativity is available through STARTHROWER, 26 East Exchange St., Suite 600, St. Paul, MN 55101 and also at www.starthrower.com.

60. See chapter 6, "The Way Forward in Mission" (p. 36), regarding the significance of being rooted in the neighborhood; Fain, *From Place of Purpose*, 12.

We know the Shepherd. We were created to participate in Jesus' saving mission for all the earth. If we are the hands and feet of Christ in the world, as Theresa of Avila writes, what is our witness? What are we teaching others about the Good Shepherd who leads us? Are there lost sheep in our own parish? When we encounter people at work or school, at the soccer field or golf course, will they know we are Christians by our love, by the way we care for one another, for the least of these, for the lost? At the end of the day, we fail to follow if we do not live the incarnate love we proclaim.[61]

As the exercises concluded, the vestry and other leaders gathered to sort, analyze, and honor every commitment and piece of wisdom contributed at each of the five events. While a standard development of a strategic plan was not the intention of this process, the development of a strategic vision was intentional. Using a series of questions that sorted and grouped the wisdom of the people, the vestry developed this statement:

The People of God of the Church of the Good Shepherd desire to join with God in His redemptive mission in the world. We humbly and prayerfully seek His grace in this journey which honors Jesus Christ as the center of our communal, familial, and individual lives. We understand that our life together is shaped by these signs gathered from prayerful and guided discernment:

- We will grow in our discipleship and in our willingness to encourage others in their own discipleship of Jesus Christ.
- We offer our lives as active partners in God's mission, remembering that we are people blessed with an amazing array of gifts and abilities to bless others.
- We seek out those who are lost or left out for caring service and to hear Good News of Jesus, the Good Shepherd.
- We stand on an Anglican heritage and traditions that guide and shape our common life, ministry, and mission for today.
- We sustain children and young people and their families, and those of every generation, striving together to know, love, and serve our Lord Jesus.[62]

From these principles the vestry began to discern the next steps to make the vision operative in the daily life of the Church of the Good Shepherd and her people. Some of those steps included a flattening of the organizational pyramid, recognizing the people of God as the ministers of the church and the clergy and other leaders as servants who equip the people for their ministry. The ministry of the staff and leaders becomes one of encouraging and preparing the people to answer God's call to be sent into the world in witness to God's love. This process is engaged in three ways as the people of God: (1)

---

61. Fain, *From Place of Purpose*, 17.
62. Fain, *From Place of Purpose*, 19.

are built up in the church community as disciples, (2) engage in caring service in the community, and (3) share the Good News of Jesus.

"The word used to describe those congregations that are attempting to shift their emphasis from program to people, from being church focused to kingdom focused, moving from Christendom assumptions about ministry to those suited for the new apostolic era is *missional*," says Robert Fain. "Missional congregations are preparing the people of God for caring service to others motivated by God's love and for sharing Good News of Jesus with others as the Holy Spirit leads and gives opportunity to do so. Good Shepherd aspires to be a missional congregation." The church is now in the process of finding ways to build disciples in the church and send them into the world as apostles.[63]

What about their energy level? It is growing. Even the old Christendom markers are changing as attendance increases. They mark their journey with the words of Julian of Norwich, speaking of Jesus working in her life:

> I can make all things well;
> I will make all things well;
> I shall make all things well;
> and thou canst see for thyself
> that all manner of
> things shall be well.[64]

---

63. Robert Fain has chronicled this process in a booklet entitled *From Place of Purpose to People of Purpose*. Copies are available by contacting The Church of the Good Shepherd, 200 Walton Way, Augusta, GA 30904.

64. Fain, *From Place of Purpose*, 26.

Works Consulted

Archbishop's Council on Mission and Public Affairs. *Mission-Shaped Church: Church Planting and Fresh Expressions in a Changing Context.* New York: Seabury Books, 2009.

Bass, Diana Butler. *The Practicing Congregation: Imagining a New Old Church.* Herndon, VA: Alban Institute, 2004.

Bass, Diana Butler, and Joseph Stewart-Sicking. *From Nomads to Pilgrims: Stories from Practicing Congregations.* Herndon, VA: Alban Institute, 2006.

†Boren, M. Scott. *Missional Small Groups: Becoming a Community That Makes a Difference in the World.* Grand Rapids: Baker Books, 2010.

†Brafman, Ori, and Rod Beckstrom. *The Starfish and the Spider: The Unstoppable Power of Leaderless Organizations.* New York: Penguin Group, 2006.

†Branson, Mark Lau. *Memories, Hopes and Conversations: Appreciative Inquiry and Congregational Change.* Herndon, VA: Alban Institute, 2004.

Campbell, Dennis G. *Congregations as Learning Communities: Tools for Shaping Your Future.* Bethesda, MD: Alban Institute, 2000.

Chait, Richard, William P. Ryan, and Barbara E. Taylor. *Governance as Leadership.* Hoboken, NJ: Wiley & Sons, 2005.

Church of England. *Mission-Shaped Church.* London: Church House Publishing, 2004.

de Bary, Edward O. *Theological Reflection: The Creation of Spiritual Power in the Information Age.* Collegeville, MN: Liturgical Press, 2003.

Easum, William M. *Sacred Cows Make Gourmet Burgers.* Nashville: Abingdon Press, 1995.

Fain, Robert. *From Place of Purpose to People of Purpose.* Augusta, GA: Church of the Good Shepherd, 2011.

†Geoffrion, Timothy C. *The Spirit-Led Leader: Nine Leadership Practices and Soul Principles.* Herndon, VA: Alban Institute, 2005.

Greenleaf, Robert K. *Servant Leadership: A Journey into the Nature of Legitimate Power and Greatness.* Mahwah, NJ: Paulist Press, 2002.

†Grenz, Linda L. *Transforming Disciples.* New York: Church Publishing, 2008.

Guder, Darrell L., ed. *Missional Church: A Vision for the Sending of the Church in North America.* Grand Rapids: Eerdmans, 1998.

Halverstadt, Hugh F. *Managing Church Conflict.* Louisville: Westminster John Knox Press, 1991.

Heifetz, Ronald A., and Marty Linsky. *Leadership on the Line.* Boston: Harvard Business School Press, 2002.

†Hotchkiss, Dan. *Governance and Ministry: Rethinking Board Leadership.* Herndon, VA: Alban Institute, 2004.

Johnson, Abigail. *Reflecting with God: Connecting Faith and Daily Life in Small Groups.* Herndon, VA: Alban Institute, 2004.

†Keifert, Patrick. *We Are Here Now: A New Missional Era.* Eagle, ID: Allelon Publishing, 2006.

Lamb, Larry F., and Kathy Brittain McKee. *Applied Public Relations: Cases in Stakeholder Management.* Mahwah, NJ: Lawrence Erlbaum Associates, 2005.

†Lemler, James. *Transforming Congregations.* New York: Church Publishing, 2008.

†Mead, Loren, *Five Challenges of the Once and Future Church.* Herndon, VA: Alban Institute, 1996.

†Mead, Loren. *The Once and Future Church: Reinventing the Church for the New Mission Frontier.* Herndon, VA: Alban Institute, 1991.

†Mead, Loren. *Transforming Congregations for the Future.* Herndon, VA: Alban Institute, 1994.

†McNeal, Reggie. *Missional Renaissance: Changing the Scorecard for the Church.* San Francisco: Jossey-Bass, 2009.

†McNeal, Reggie. *The Present Future: Six Tough Questions for the Church.* San Francisco, Jossey-Bass, 2003.

Mitchell, Glen John. *Educating Anglican Clergy as Missional Leaders: The Context and the Challenges of the Twenty-first Century.* Vancouver: Vancouver School of Theology, 2010.

Murray, Stuart. *Post-Christendom: Church and Mission in a Strange New World.* Carlisle, PA: Paternoster, 2004.

Nelson, Randolph A. "Congregations in the New Century." *Word and Word* XX, no. 4 (Fall 2000).

Nouwen, Henri. "Moving from Solitude to Community." *Leadership Journal* (Spring 1995).

Reed, Bruce. *The Dynamics of Religion: Process and Movement in Christian Churches.* London: Darton, Longman and Todd, 1978.

†Roxburgh, Alan J., and Fred Romanuk. *Introducing the Missional Church: What It Is, Why It Matters, How to Become One.* Grand Rapids: Baker Books, 2009.

†Roxburgh, Alan J., and M. Scott Boren. *The Missional Leader: Equipping Your Church to Reach a Changing World*. San Francisco: Jossey-Bass, 2006.

†Scott, Katherine Tyler. *Transforming Leadership*. New York: Church Publishing, 2010.

Senge, Peter M. *The Fifth Discipline: The Art and Practice of the Learning Organization*. New York: Currency Doubleday, 1994.

Sitze, Bob. *The Great Permission*. Chicago: Evangelical Lutheran Church in America, 2002.

†Snow, Luther. *The Power of Asset Mapping: How Your Congregation Can Act on Its Gifts*. Herndon, VA: Alban Institute, 2004.

Strommen, Merton P. *The Innovative Church*. Minneapolis: Augsburg Fortress, 1997.

Swagerty, Lois. *Taking Your Church Missional*. Leadership Network, undated. Online resource at www.leadnet.org.

Tickle, Phyllis. *The Great Emergence: How Christianity Is Changing and Why*. Grand Rapids: Baker Books, 2008.

Van Gelder, Craig, ed.. *The Missional Church and Denominations: Helping Congregations Develop a Missional Identity*. Grand Rapids: Eerdmans, 2008.

Van Gelder, Craig, and Dwight Zscheile. *The Missional Church in Perspective: Mapping Trends and Shaping the Conversation*. Grand Rapids: Baker Academic, 2011.

†Zscheile, Dwight J. *People of the Way: Renewing Episcopal Identity*. New York: Morehouse Publishing, 2012.

† = recommended for vestry and leadership group discussion

PART TWO
Resources

Many of the resources in this section have been gathered over the years without publication in mind. Though every effort has been made to trace down all sources, if an attribution is missing, please accept my apologies and be assured of correction in subsequent editions.

Movements and Shifts in the Church of Today

There is an exploding collection of literature that tries to observe and explain the movements and shifts the people of God are experiencing in these times. Some are beginning to name this period the New Apostolic Era. As well, there is a developing consensus among these observers that considers the church's and the believer's transformation through and in each of these shifts or movements.[64]

From the Center to the Margins

The Christian story and the churches were central in Christendom. The effect of Constantine's acceptance and promotion of Christianity placed the church at the center of the empire's cultural and political processes. As the relationship evolved, the distinction between the institutional church and the state were blurred, with each holding on to the significant trappings of power and prestige. In the rise of monarchies in the West, privilege was locked in place through the establishment of state churches. In the United States, though enshrining separation of church and state in law, there was a *de facto* establishment of Christianity until the middle of the twentieth century.

In this emerging era, the church and its people are moving to the edges, to the margins. The symbiotic relationship of the church blessing culture and the culture blessing the church is breaking down. While living at the center, the church helped train respectable citizens who helped maintain the boundaries

---

64. This list follows Murray Stuart in *Post-Christendom: Church and Mission in a Strange New World* (Milton Keynes, UK: Paternoster, 2004), 20, but is noted by many others with variation.

and institutions of society. Though there still exists much God talk in the political arena, these acknowledgements of the divine are not much more than
platitudes used to appeal to residual faith bases. The church's move today is
from being an influential core of society to a position on the sidelines.[65]

From Being the Majority to Being the Minority

In Christendom, Christians were the majority (often overwhelmingly) and in
the world of today (at least in the Western world), Christians are more and
more becoming a minority. The number of those who participate in worship
services is slipping. A majority of Europeans and North Americans do not attend services in houses of worship. It has also been noted that those who do
attend worship are doing so less frequently.[66]

The external cultural endorsement and encouragement toward participation in the life of a congregation is virtually nonexistent in most places and
significantly diminished in the remainder. The latest peak of participation followed World War II, and the mainline churches have been in steady decline
for decades as Christians move from majority to minority.

From Being Settlers to Being Pioneers
and Journeyers

In a culture shaped by their values and story, Christendom Christians felt
at home. Centuries of being settled into an accommodation with the surrounding culture have formed a particular shape of church that has enjoyed
acceptance and entitlement. Tax exemption, Sunday time-encroachment pro-
tection, status, and in some countries state establishment allowed churches to
put down roots and thrive through their cooperation with the political system
in place in their country or state. Being settled gave a great degree of comfort,
empowerment, and certainty.

In the emerging culture, Christians are aliens, exiles, and pilgrims who feel
estranged from the succor of the old paradigm. The church is no longer in the
business of forming citizens and validating the state; discipleship no longer
equates to citizenship. Discipleship is rerooted in its primitive meaning of wit-

---

65. Walter Russell Mead, son of Loren Mead, and professor at Yale, notes this margin-
alization with his comment on the Episcopal House of Bishops: "Nobody cares what you
think while your tiny church is falling apart." (Mead's blog at *The American Interest,* February
21, 2010, http://blogs.the-american-interest.com)

66. Lovett H. Weems Jr., "No Shows: The Decline in Worship Attendance," *The Christian
Century,* September 22, 2010.

ness as being a carrier of God's blessing for the communities in which Christians live. While the culture moves more deeply into a position of neutrality or passivity about Christianity, the church shifts now from somewhat comfortable accommodation by the surrounding culture toward a more prophetic stance of working for the Good News of helping reveal the reign of God for all people.

From Privilege to Plurality

The Christendom era granted many privileges to the church and its members. Blue laws, which protected the church from the competition of Sunday commerce, have virtually disappeared. Christian prayer no longer opens meetings and classes. In the expanding marketplace, the church is only one of many structures around which people can order and make meaning of their lives. The gospel works on its own merit in the emerging era, not through any warrant by the state or culture.

The shift for the institutional church is that it is now competing with a vast array of alternatives. In the religious arena, the old-line legacy denominations are not only experiencing competition from megachurch nondenominational houses of worship,[67] but also from secular Sunday opportunities like shopping, entertainment, athletics, and staying home to relax and read the Sunday newspaper. The rise of religious pluralism also opens a widened matrix of spiritual choices. Islam has joined the other two Abrahamic faiths on American soil. There are New Age opportunities and Eastern religions like Buddhism and Confucianism. And in the last several decades, the choice expressed by "I am spiritual but not religious" has ramped up.

From Maintenance to Mission

The Christendom era, which is in the process of passing away, laid emphasis on maintaining what was viewed as the Christian status quo. One of the first mantras of the onset of this shift was that the church needed to "move from maintenance to mission." Those who caught the first breezes of the new era

---

67. Willow Creek Church, the model upon which many of these churches are based, released a study in 2008 indicating that their institutional form of church was not creating the spiritual depth their congregants seek. In an interesting alternative voice, Diana Butler Bass, based on her studies, said: "I have interviewed dozens and dozens of people throughout the United States who used to belong to churches like Willow Creek but left them in order to become Presbyterians or Lutherans or Episcopalians. Ex-members of the megachurches have sort of rediscovered a level of being Christian that they were unaware of." Diana Butler Bass, "Study Results Find Limits to Willow Creek's Model," *The Christian Index* online at www .christianindex.org.

knew that managerial church leadership styles, which looked within rather than outside, enshrined the past, and held a "come to us" rather than "go to them" approach to church life, was failing.

In this new era the growing emphasis is on mission[68] in a contested, pluralistic environment. Faithfulness reroots attentiveness to the call of the Apostolic Era: the *missio dei*, the mission of God.[69] The return to mission sees the petition of the Lord's Prayer, "Your kingdom come, your will be done, *on earth* as it is in heaven," as normative for the life of the church. The call is to let go of the comfortable, known place of the old way, and rediscover ways to live as a blessing in a world experiencing a hunger for the experience of the reign of God.

> If the Church really sees itself as the people of God, it is obvious that it can never be a static and supra-historical phenomenon, which exists undisturbed by earthly space and historical time. The Church is always and everywhere a living people, gathered together from the peoples of this world and journeying through the midst of time. The Church is essentially en route, on a journey, a pilgrimage. A Church which pitches its tents without looking out constantly for new horizons, which does not continually strike camp, is being untrue to its calling.
>
> —Hans Kung in *The Church*

From Institution to Movement

The basic mode of Christians in the Christendom era was institutional with hierarchical structure.[70] The nature of an institution is to have rules, regulations, and approved systems and procedures. Power is centralized and standards—be they monarchial or somewhat democratic—guard the entry into its corps of leaders. Much focus is backward looking in order to preserve the gains the institution has made in the past.

In the post-Christendom era, the organizational modality is returning to its original form as a movement. The earliest days of the church were marked with a clear message and vision, which impelled the followers of Christ forward in space and time. This compelling, constitutive vision of wholeness and freedom took hold of early Christians so thoroughly that they organized their lives around it and were willing to die to keep it alive. The power of the church

---

68. The Prayer Book definition of mission in the Catechism is "The mission of the Church is to restore all people to unity with God and each other in Christ," 855.

69. See Craig Van Gelder, ed., *The Missional Church and Denominations: Helping Congregations Develop a Missional Identity* (Grand Rapids: Wm. B. Eerdmans, 2008), 161–63, for a succinct discussion of *missio dei* written by Dwight Zscheile. See the whole chapter, entitled "A More True 'Domestic and Foreign Missionary Society': Toward a Missional Polity for the Episcopal Church," for a helpful discourse on a rerooted polity for the church.

70. This would be true, though to a lesser degree, of the churches born out of the more radical Reformation, including Baptists, Congregationalists, and other evangelicals.

as a movement, before there existed law and hierarchy, was in its generosity, generatively, and adaptability.

Comparing the characteristics of the first centuries of the church's life and the present day uncovers many similarities, the most significant of which is living as a minority in a culture that is, at its best, indifferent and, at its worst, hostile. In an age referred to as the Apostolic Age of the church and this present-day experience of the church that may be called the New Apostolic Age, it is mission that is energizing the church. The focus is not inward, but rather outward for the sake of the world.

These basic paradigmatic shifts thread their way throughout this book. Next, we turn to some of the institutions that may need some reinvention for the church to be vital in the twenty-first century and beyond.

Change and More Change

The picture painted in this book may give the impression that the time the church has spent on the earth may be divided into three discrete periods: The Apostolic Era covering the time of Christ to the Edict of Milan in the early fourth century, the Constantinian or Christendom Era from Constantine to the twentieth century, and the New Apostolic Era from the twentieth century until now. Eras and epochs and their origin and terminus are the stuff of historical debate.

Those who lived a century apart in ancient Greece would not likely have experienced significant differences in the daily course of their lives. Great-great-great-grandchildren who lived in feudal Europe led lives very much like their foreparents. This is not the case for those who live today. Rapid change is our companion.

The onset of change we now experience is so new that it is often described or named by what it is not: post-Christian or post-Constantinian or postmodern. To visualize this change, imagine a timeline that stretches back into the Middle Ages from the turn of the second millennium. The line moves from light to dark with light representing little noticeable change and dark representing significant noticeable change. The line begins as almost imperceptibly gray in the Middle Ages. The institutionalized Christendom church has been the experience of Western culture for a thousand years. The introduction of gray along the line represents the introduction of modern influences.[71]

> Christendom is a series of compromises made by the church with the world so that the offense of Jesus Christ is watered down, mitigated, and obscured to the point that the world is satisfied that the church is no longer foreign and dangerous.
>
> —Craig Carter in *Rethinking Christ and Culture*

---

71. The Modern Era is marked by the rise of capitalism, industrialization, advances in science, technology, and the arts, denominationalism, and colonialism.

By the middle of the seventeenth century and the rise of the Modern Era, pre-modern people had experienced change in a minimal way and the church as a core, stabilizing institution in culture. In the Modern Era, change picks up its pace and over this period of time it would have become perceptible to the average person.

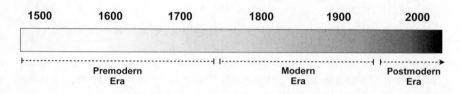

Look at the timeline in the middle of the twentieth century. At the century's beginning it is lighter gray, but in rapid order the color moves toward black. Gray (in all its shades) on this timeline is the color of Christendom. Black is the color of this new era that is so new (fifty or so years old) that there is no agreement on a name for these times. On the timeline, lighter shades of gray are almost gone and what we see are darker and darker grays that are moving toward black. Some of this change is so noticeable that it is happening before our eyes. Most people of faith who are more than a couple of decades old can testify to the change they observe in the church.

It is this change, with more to come, that is a significant and abiding context of leadership in the twenty-first century.

RESOURCE B
Vestry Meetings
This source also available online.

Implied in the ten functions explored in this book is a particular way to gather and meet as the vestry. In this new era the vestry and all leader groups will seek to give the congregation the gift of missional leadership. This resource looks at the shape of the meeting of a vestry whose desire is to be a missional leadership council. The governance functions in this agenda are concentrated, allowing greater time for the development of an atmosphere of discipleship formation in the church so that the people will be equipped to serve the world in the name of Christ.

In this resource section you will find:

• a suggested order of meeting

• how to organize the school of leadership

• a retreat format

❧

A Suggested Order of Meeting

30 MINUTES
Gathering: Bible Study and Prayer *see the suggested forms*

0 MINUTES
Minutes

• "approved" as distributed with corrections received at any time

5–10 MINUTES
Financial Report

- use language accessible to all with an executive summary
- person reporting should highlight key points and any actionable items
- a norm to be honored is highly focused discussion
- general financial positions may be discussed here or in Discipleship or Mission time

10–15 MINUTES
Discipleship

- programmatic activity of the parish that forms disciples: worship, formation, fellowship, and generosity (stewardship)
- receive and discuss any discipleship-related reports
- matters pending from previous meetings pertaining to discipleship

15–30 MINUTES
Mission

- actions that send the baptized into the world (apostleship): service, financial support, evangelism, social justice
- receive and discuss any mission-related reports
- matters pending from previous meetings pertaining to mission

0–10 MINUTES
Other Items Needing Vestry Attention

- this is the catch-all time of the meeting
- anything that doesn't fit elsewhere
- other actionable items pending from previous meetings

30 MINUTES
Leadership School

- leadership development is the focus of this segment
- time for study and reflection (see resource section)

1 MINUTE
Sending

- personal and corporate mission is primed by being sent into the world to be a blessing

Notes

1. If every element of this order of meeting went to the maximum suggested time, the meeting would take about two hours. Note that is a maximum time-frame; ninety minutes is a more likely timeframe. It may be helpful to appoint a process observer in the implementation of this schedule. The observer, a member of the vestry, simply pays attention to the flow of the meeting, verbally marks the passage of time, and reports on her or his process observations at the end of the meeting. Some vestries find it helpful for the clerk to verbally note the hour and half-hour elapsed time. As well, this time framework helps remove the possibility of micromanagement so that the vestry may concentrate on the big view, the overall vitality of the church.

2. It is very likely that this Order of Meeting will need to be gradually implemented. The four key elements—Bible Study, Tending to Discipleship, Raising Up Apostles (mission activity), and the School of Leadership—may be introduced in this way:

- Continue your present practice of opening devotions and prayer.

- Ask half the vestry to focus attention to *discipleship* formation within your normal meeting format; ask the other half to be attentive listeners for *mission* activity. Add the School of Leadership time at the end. Before entering the School of Leadership portion of the meeting, ask the listeners to report on what they heard through focused attention. This action begins to form the attention of members of the vestry. Note that many parts of a discussion may actually have both missional (or apostolic) and discipleship as components. Attention will likely be drawn to parts of parish life that reflect neither.

3. All items brought before the vestry requiring action (except for emergencies) are placed on a thirty-or-more-day clock. This practice is that no action be taken on items introduced for the first time. Consequently, two gifts are given: there is no tyranny of urgency and time is amplified to ponder the step. This would include, for example, a finance report. Those who have ideas about what is presented at one vestry meeting can seek details in the intervening time and be prepared to accept the report (as is or modified) at the next meeting.

4. When a decision is made, especially those that might be referred to as actionable items, it is a good practice to append a simple list to the minutes of any open or not yet accomplished item. This list is visited regularly during the "other items" section of the meeting for purposes of accountability and tracking. These actionable items may also be considered, as appropriate, in the Discipleship section or Mission section. The key point here is that important decisions be provided support and follow-through.

5. Consensus formation is the recommended model for decision making. In an action that is pro forma, consensus may be noted simply by anyone saying, "I propose that the vestry accept this report by consensus." The chair then asks if there is consensus, "Is this the mind of the vestry?" Members of the vestry then give their assent (or not). For decision making that is not pro forma, see the fuller discussion of consensus in chapter 3.

6. Reports from members of the vestry or others who have worked for the good of the church's ministries and mission are always received gratefully and, if action is required, with a predisposition to say yes to what is presented or requested. This is the nature of a permission-giving church; it seeks to offer creative space for the work of the Spirit in others. More information is found in part H of this resource section, "A Primer on Permission-Giving Churches" (p. 112). The vestry should inform all who are bringing reports or requests before the vestry that require action about the thirty-day clock on taking action.

7. An extension of being a permission-giving church is captured in the question, does it need to come before the vestry? When a church is dedicated to the extension of the Gospel of Jesus Christ, there will be many nudges from the Spirit that call the baptized into service. The vestry will find itself, when it is missional, more in the mode of simple gratitude and less in the mode of being an agency of authorization and validation. The vestry should expect to move higher and higher in its oversight, thus vacating any need to micromanage.

8. The desired movement is to leave behind inordinate attention to governance and open up space for generative discussion. Bible study will prepare the way for such discussion by engagement with the narrative of our faith. The general discussion at a meeting of the vestry is reframed into a double focus: discipleship formation and mission, which is the daily service of all the baptized of pointing to the inbreaking reign of God through word and deed to their neighbors.

9. There is a sinkhole into which any vestry or leadership team can fall. It is called "scarcity." There is no room on the agenda for a bottom-dwelling lament. All time spent in scarcity is energy depleting. If the vestry cannot quickly find a creative response to the challenges that pull it down into lament, it is strongly recommended that you go to your bishop and ask for assistance. One of the reasons we have bishops is to connect us to a body larger than we are. Every parish—no matter the size—needs assistance beyond their present capacity from time to time. The resources in this book that will help avoid the scarcity sinkhole are "Appreciative Inquiry Primer" (p. 93) and "Introduction to Asset-Based Ministry" (p. 98).

Organizing the School of Leadership

As noted in chapter 10 and in this Vestry Meetings resource, the vestry meeting and its activities create an opportunity for formation in missional leadership. The key point here is to always include a time for leadership development. The gift of forming and fitting leaders is not only for service in the church's ministry but also offers useful grounding for leaders in their daily lives.

This book is divided into ten chapters. Each of the chapters concludes with pointers to additional resources and discussion questions. In the three-year leadership training cycle that follows, there is a recommended sequence of using this book for one of the years of the cycle. In the next year, the recommended reading is Dwight Zscheile's *People of the Way*. Dr. Zscheile provides a theologically informed saga to light the path for missional engagement.

The third year of the cycle has a dual recommendation, both from Church Publishing's "Transforming Church" series. The first is Katherine Tyler Scott's *Transforming Leadership* and the second is *Transforming Disciples* by Linda Grenz. Both books are profound in their simplicity and offer helpful discussion questions for each chapter.

As the knowledge base, leadership skills, and missional commitment multiply, share the learnings with the whole parish through classes, forums, and action.

Vestries are selected to serve the congregation on a three-year rotation. As you embark upon your own version of leadership formation on your vestry, keep in mind that each year one-third of the membership will change. Determine ways to bring new members into the group and its missional perspective. One simple method is to have a member who is completing a term to spend some time with the person taking his or her seat. Alternatively, you may find a review time useful at your annual retreat.

The books marked with a *dagger* [†] in the list of Works Consulted (p. 69) will be useful as texts in your vestry leadership school. In the summer, when many vestries meet less frequently, use one of these books as a summer reading project with the vestry.

A Syllabus for Three-Year Cycle of Study follows. The three-year cycle is repeatable, allowing all members to experience the content over a three-year period of service on the vestry. This is a recommended sequence. You may rearrange the format to best accommodate your leadership group. If the vestry uses the alternative format suggested below (Vestry Retreat plus Vestry Workday), consider opening up the experience to additional parish leaders.

Syllabus for a Three-Year Cycle of Study	Year One	Year Two	Year Three
Month 1	Chapters 1 & 10* *Cultivating the Missional Church*	Introduction** *People of the Way* by Zscheile	Chapter 2*** *Transforming Leadership* by Scott
Month 2	Chapter 9 *Cultivating the Missional Church*	Chapter 1 *People of the Way* by Zscheile	Chapter 3 *Transforming Leadership* by Scott
Month 3	Chapter 6 *Cultivating the Missional Church*	Chapter 2 *People of the Way* by Zscheile	Chapter 4 *Transforming Leadership* by Scott
Month 4	Chapter 2 *Cultivating the Missional Church*	Chapter 3 *People of the Way* by Zscheile	Chapter 5 *Transforming Leadership* by Scott
Month 5	Chapter 3 *Cultivating the Missional Church*	Chapter 4 *People of the Way* by Zscheile	Chapter 1 *Transforming Disciples* by Grenz
Month 6	Chapter 4 *Cultivating the Missional Church*	Chapter 5 *People of the Way* by Zscheile	Chapter 2 *Transforming Disciples* by Grenz
Month 7	Chapters 5 *Cultivating the Missional Church*	Chapter 6 *People of the Way* by Zscheile	Chapter 3 *Transforming Disciples* by Grenz
Month 8	Chapter 7 *Cultivating the Missional Church*	Chapter 7 *People of the Way* by Zscheile	Chapter 4 *Transforming Disciples* by Grenz
Month 9	Chapter 8 *Cultivating the Missional Church*	Congregational Life Cycle (resource section)	Chapter 5 *Transforming Disciples* by Grenz
Month 10	Core Learnings of the Year	Core Learnings of the Year	Core Learnings of the Year
	* Everyone should read the prologue of this book as background. *** New members should also read the prologue of this book.* **** Chapter 1 reconsiders information in the prologue in this book.*		

In year one of the syllabus, the selections are from this book and are offered with a recommended chapter sequence. Be sure to include in your discussions the additional resources in part two when recommended by a chapter. In many cases the resources in part two give an introduction to an approach that you will want to introduce beyond the leadership team. Parish study groups, Lenten evenings, ECW, and men's group meetings will benefit from members of the vestry leading presentations from their learnings. Some of these resources are downloadable and reproducible at www.churchpublishing.org/cultivatingthemissionalchurch.

This ten-month calendar assumes that the vestry may not meet during vacation months. If you have additional full meetings of the vestry in a year, redistribute the chapter assignments, add studies from part two of this book, or take a break.

Each of the books in this syllabus is available from Church Publishing Incorporated and has an integrated study guide.

This is a recommended cycle of study. You may find other resources more suited to your circumstance. In years two and three, substitute any book or resource that builds leaders and deepens missional commitment in your congregation. Take special note of the books in the list of Works Consulted (p. 69) marked with a dagger (†) for other options.

An alternative to the monthly Syllabus for a Three-Year Cycle of Study model suggested is to use a Vestry Retreat plus Vestry Workday model. The format is that the vestry year begins with a retreat utilizing months 1–5 or 6 of the above cycle during the retreat. The remaining blocks, including the "Core Learnings" exercise, become the content of a (Saturday, perhaps) workday six months later. This model assumes that the same members of the vestry are at both gatherings. Should you choose this alternative format, consider using the theological reflection model in the available time space during your vestry meetings.

Core Learnings Excercise

As part of your study, have the clerk record the big ideas that arise in each block of study. This may be done simply and quickly through a brief idea collection at the end of each portion of a meeting.[72] These big ideas are principles, concepts, learnings, operational modes, suggestions, steps to take, guidelines, and any other information that deserves to be honored and remembered in congregational life. The ideas should be succinct. Half a sentence is the recommended length. They might also be recorded on newsprint and kept posted in the vestry meeting room.

---

72. "Big Ideas" may appear at any time during a meeting. When a principle surfaces in a meeting, take note of if for use in this exercise.

At the last meeting of the year, all the big ideas are posted. Affinities are noted and similar ideas grouped. There is no right number; it could be a few dozen or a hundred. When affinity grouping is complete, distill your big ideas into no more than five to seven groupings. Give each group a name and create a list of groups. Label each item on your list as a principle/learning or an actionable item. For a principle/learning, determine how it will be grounded in the parish. If it is an actionable item, determine the "who, what, when, where, why, how" of the action. For everything determined to have value for the church, choose a time for the vestry to revisit each item for carry-through and a means to communicate this valued principle or action to the congregation.

A helpful overlay to focus the group on priorities is to ask three questions: (1) Is it a fundamental practice, proposed action, or principle of this church that is essential to our life together? (2) Is it a good thing but not a fundamental practice or principle for mission and ministry? (3) Is it optional or nonessential to our life as a congregation? Use consensus to determine how you categorize your principles and proposed actions. It is worth noting that institutional Christendom churches could get tied up in the "tyranny of the good" by doing (too) many good things that detract from the congregation's primary purpose and focus as participants in God's mission. The answer to the third question will beg another question: What is it that may need to be released so that the congregation may be highly focused on God's essential mission?

The core learning exercise may need more time than a regular vestry meeting.

Vestry Retreats

Those who serve on vestries want to know how to focus and harness their individual and collective gifts to build or keep vitality in their congregation. Retreats serve this purpose well. Here are some things to keep in mind when planning a vestry retreat to support and extend healthy leadership in the congregation:

- Choose a place apart from the church. Conference centers are a great choice. Parishioner vacation homes can be an economical alternative. The beauty of nature has a way of letting the hand of God work silently.

- Seek full participation from the vestry. For perspective, it is sometimes helpful to widen the circle to include, for example, youth representatives, retiring members, former wardens, and leaders of various ministries.

- Resourced parishes may engage a retreat leader who has skills in vestry ministry. Those with limited resources may ask for a leader from the diocese. Any vestry can also forego having a leader by using, for example, a selection of articles from *Vestry Papers*, now available online (www.episcopalfoundation.org) for presentation at the retreat. While visiting the Foundation's website, peruse the large compilation of resources found there.

- Any retreat should be wrapped in prayer. Consider giving the vestry a Scripture passage to reflect on in advance and utilize in Bible studies and liturgies during the retreat. Begin or end celebrating a Eucharist with the homily time previewing or summarizing the time together.

- Plan for at least twenty-four hours together. Longer retreats (36 or 48 hours) allow more time for interaction and development. A good schedule allows for gathering, worship, presentation/discussion, meals, free time, and commissioning/sending. In addition to the annual retreat, consider scheduling a mini-retreat midway through the year.

- Allowing ample time for conversation, friendship, and play builds camaraderie, trust, and cohesion.

- Content is a highly variable element of a retreat. Save the business for another time or at least concentrate it into a brief session. Presentations and experiences form a common ground that all share. The point here is that every member of the vestry brings a rich experience of leadership in the world. The church is a different place where new skills and approaches, sometimes at odds with the world, are used and may need to be learned. Some worthwhile content for a retreat might include:

  1. using this book as the content for a retreat, reading *Asset Mapping* by Luther Snow, and previewing its use in the parish at the retreat

  2. using storytelling to remember spiritually significant times in the church

  3. learning Appreciative Inquiry processes (see Rob Voyle's "Vestry Interview Guide" at www.clergyleadership.com)

  4. reading any book by Loren Mead (see "Works Consulted," p. 69) and working with his ideas for your future

  5. attending a vestry or leadership retreat at a church conference center

- Retreats are key times in which to establish the culture of the vestry and the way it embodies the reign of God, honoring Jesus' words that he came bringing abundant life. There are well-worn paths to both a depreciative culture as well as paths to health and abundance. The vestry chooses the path. Use the retreat to honor that which you value.

• Finally, if there is any overt or covert besetting conflict in the church or on the vestry, it is of supreme importance that an outside consultant be engaged. Resourced parishes may engage a consultant; churches with limited resources will find assistance through the diocesan office.

Baptism is the origin and source of all ministry. The ministry of a vestry serves as a beacon in every church to shed light on and be energized by the gifts of the Spirit given in baptism. It is an ongoing process in every vestry to lead in discerning and encouraging the form and face of the reign of God in the place they serve. Vestry retreats are food for this journey.

The Principle of Subsidiarity[73]

The character of the Christian faith from its early days has given it a profound investment in the quality of personal, face-to-face relationships. Christians are called to embody in daily life God's reconciliation of all things in Christ, living newly in the light of God's justice and forgiveness. It is through the personal witness of Christians to the reality of that new life that the attractiveness of the gospel becomes apparent. And the gifts of the Holy Spirit, which are various to different people, are given precisely so that, used together in humility and love and with attentiveness to one another's interests, they may contribute to the building up of the whole body.

The principle of subsidiarity has been formulated to express this investment in the local and face-to-face. Properly used, subsidiarity means "a central authority should have a subsidiary function, performing only those tasks which cannot be performed effectively at a more immediate or local level" (Oxford English Dictionary).

Subsidiarity may properly be applied to the life of the church in order to resist the temptation of centralism. But in the life of the church the local level was never seen as simply autonomous. Because the work of Christ was itself a reconciliation of humanity, there is evidence from the first days of the church of concern for the unity of the communities. St. Paul, for example, writes of his anxiety for the continuity of preaching and teaching the authentic apostolic gospel and for the effectiveness of the united witness of the church to the gospel of reconciliation. Care was taken, as the church grew, to preserve

---

73. Condensed from *The Virginia Report* (London: Anglican Consultative Council by the Secretary General, 1997), chap. 4.

the continuity of its witness across time and its coherence and effectiveness in different places.

It is important to clarify the principles that should govern the relationships within the life of the church. Clarity on this matter makes for creative, sustainable, and transparent partnerships in the body of Christ. Every "higher" authority ought to encourage the free use of God's gifts at "lower" levels. There must be clarity on what has to be observed and carried out at every level, and also on the limits of its competence. As much space as possible should be given to personal initiative and responsibility.

Anglicans may properly claim that the observation of different levels and the granting of considerable freedom to the lowest possible level has been a feature of their polity.

RESOURCE D
Appreciative Inquiry Primer

Billy raced out the front door and slammed it behind him. BLAM! He ran down the sidewalk toward the church with its big side yard. He was off to play baseball, and he couldn't wait to get started. His parents had given him a new bat for his eleventh birthday. This was his first chance to try it out. His friend BJ joined him at the corner.

It was going to be a great day. Billy held the bat high for his friend to admire, as BJ reached out his hand to hold it. Then, suddenly the bat slipped out of their hands and right into the plate glass window of Gaston's Drug Store, owned by BJ's next-door neighbor.

Disaster. The boys stared at the awful hole in the window. Each wished he were somewhere else. Everyone on the block came running. They thought about running, but couldn't move. They just stood there staring at the drug store window display with its bottles and boxes and thousands of tiny pieces of glass. And lying in the middle of it all—the brand new bat. The boys knew that people were all around them, but they could not look up.

Then the boys heard one gruff voice above all the others. Somebody was standing right next to them. "Hey," the voice said. "BJ, what have you done? You are always messing up. I'd expect something stupid of you. Billy, what are you doing with this little jerk? Who's going to pay for this?" BJ was embarrassed and Billy felt awful.

"Who's going to take care of this?" Mr. Gaston almost yelled again.

Billy opened his mouth to speak, but nothing came out.

Then, just when all the sounds around him were getting jumbled up together, Billy heard a voice he knew.

"Billy is mine. He is a good boy." It was his dad. Billy looked up to see his father standing next to him.

"I'll pay for the window," said his dad, putting his hand on Billy's shoulder and pulling him close.

BJ looked at his buddy and thought about the trouble he would get in when he got home.[74]

Which young man do you think will have a childhood that builds a strong, healthy future?

The simple truth is that we are at our best when we focus on that which is positive, appreciative, and life giving rather than tending to that which is negative and depreciating.

Appreciative Inquiry is such an approach to community development, large or small, that generates trust, vitality, vision, and an enthusiastic sense of shared purpose and engagement. It was created as a way to analyze and learn, moving a group toward understanding, discovery, and innovation.

> I give you a new commandment, that you love one another. Just as I have loved you, you also should love one another.
>
> —John 13:34

> Appreciative Inquiry is the study and exploration of what gives life to human systems when they function at their best. This approach to personal change and organization change is based on the assumption that questions and dialogue about strengths, successes, values, hopes, and dreams are themselves transformational. In short, Appreciative Inquiry suggests that human organizing and change, at its best, is a relational process of inquiry, grounded in affirmation and appreciation.[75]
>
> . . . If taken deeply enough, appreciative processes of knowing and interaction enlarge our sense of solidarity with others, overcome the arrogance of prejudice and cultural blindness, and allow for the cooperative evolution of the shared values, accountabilities, and meanings that shape the collective good.[76]

Appreciative Inquiry was developed as an alternative to problem solving. Instead of focusing on what does not work (i.e., a problem), it pays special attention to . . .

• our gifts,

• our values and what we value most (for instance, our church, family, or vocation)

• the most vital, enlivening experiences we've had and what we can learn from them

---

74. This story was inspired by one told by the late Urban T. Holmes.

75. Diana Whitney and Amanda Trosten-Bloom, *The Power of Appreciative Inquiry: A Practical Guide to Positive Change* (San Francisco: Berrett-Koehler, 2003), 1.

76. David Cooperrider and Suresh Srivastva, "Appreciative Inquiry in Organizational Life," *Research in Organizational Change and Development*, 1 (1987): 129–69

- the images and opportunities that most capture our imagination
- our deepest yearnings for what we might become

Appreciative Inquiry literally does what it says. It focuses on our blessings, what we are thankful for and appreciate. Then it goes to work inquiring and learning about cultivating those blessings to their full potential.

Those who use Appreciative Inquiry and its exercises create a sense of safety and trust, because instead of focusing on hard, painful issues, participants share what they most enjoy and value.

Appreciative Inquiry is a research and action approach designed to empower whole systems to achieve things the community never dreamed possible. As a whole-system approach, it seeks to be as inclusive and egalitarian as possible.

Nevertheless, learning about Appreciative Inquiry may be most personally satisfying in close one-on-one relationships, as in opening up new, trustworthy conversations between a parent and a child.

Appreciative Inquiry had its beginning at Case Western Reserve University in the early 1990s, primarily as a methodology to help corporations and institutions improve their competitive advantage or organizational effectiveness. It involves a significant shift in emphasis from problems to achievements, from participation to inspiration. By identifying and reinforcing positive and constructive actions, relationships, and visions within a faith community, Appreciative Inquiry encourages broad ownership in action taken to extend the reign of God.

Appreciative Inquiry assumes that the images we hold before us tend to shape who we become. So it mines our experience for what we think is best about our community, our gifts, and our aspirations. Along the way, it takes off the blindfolds we wear to what is possible. As a methodology, Appreciative Inquiry assumes that individuals move in the direction they study. Whether it is used inside or outside the church, an Appreciative Inquiry usually proceeds through four stages. These stages are known as the 4-D process, which can be found on pages 52–53 in chapter 9.

On the following two pages you will find a visual overview of Appreciative Inquiry.

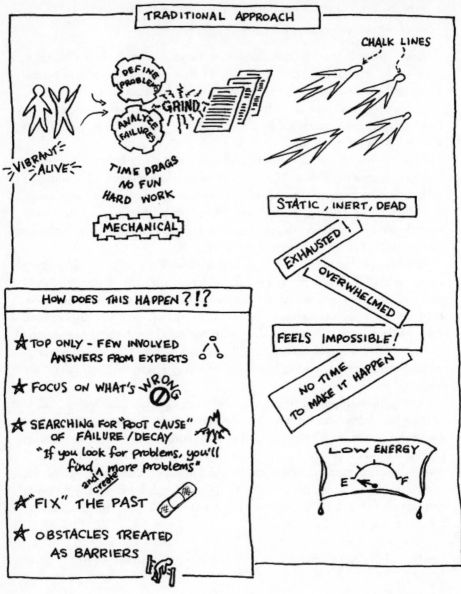

Used with permission.

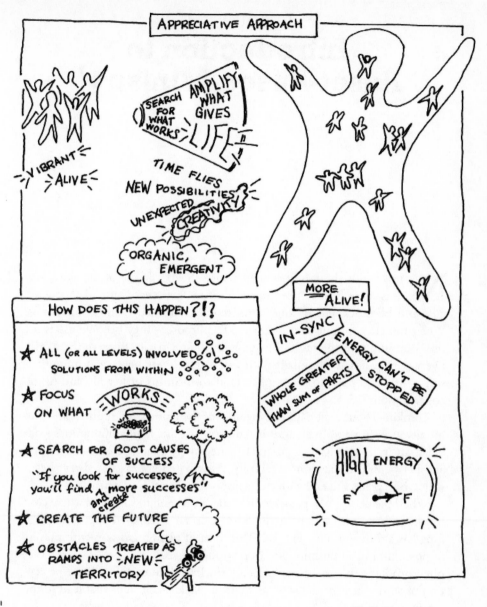

Used with permission.

Introduction to
Asset-Based Ministry[77]

N o, this is not about a financial balance sheet. The use of the word *asset* here is in its broadest sense. An asset is a gift that is useful. There are gifts and blessings, talents and competencies, knowledge and connections. When the gifts are put to use—for God's purposes—they become assets for the community of the faithful to grow in their capacity to serve the world. Every person has an abundant supply of assets. Every believer is more than sufficiently equipped to accomplish God's will in his or her life and in the congregation.[78]

Thinking about each baptized member of the church and of the faith community as a whole from an asset-based approach lifts faith communities from being stuck in scarcity and destructive negativity that can mire the church and her people in inaction or self-pity. Asset-based approaches always begin with God's grace and end with the action you take on God's behalf.

When the people of a parish look to the future and to what and where God is calling them, planning naturally follows. In an asset-based approach, planning has a different look and feel. This form of planning begins with prayers of possibilities and promise, not over-wrought neediness. Fear, the force that often produces the experience of being stuck, is diminished with the perception of sufficiency for the work as we take quick, small steps that lead to the creation and implementation of plans of what God is calling believers to accomplish together.

---

77. This article is based on the work of Luther Snow in *The Power of Asset Mapping: How Your Congregation Can Act on Its Gifts* (Herndon, VA: Alban Institute, 2004).

78. The Asset-Based Ministry process is recommended over the traditional "Time and Talent Survey" method (a common component of the Fall Every Member Canvas Fund Drive in churches).

God's abundant grace is always primary. Christian theology begins with God's creative, gracious, and loving nature made present in Jesus Christ. This abundance is purposeful. There is a flow. Blessings and gifts are only blessings and gifts *as they are given away.* God's story with humanity is one of showing graceful activity and then giving us all things needful for us to extend that grace in our churches and in our world.

This movement of grace is crystallized in what has become known as The Great Commission of "Go into the world . . . " recorded in all four gospels. This commissioning is accompanied with rich resources. God remains close at hand, not absent. The Holy Spirit empowers believers with gifts to accomplish the mission. An asset-based approach reminds God's people that they have been saved from the small- and selfish-minded notion that they are weak, powerless, or incapable of doing much more than pondering their own salvation. With the Spirit's power, God's people are capable of moving the world toward God's design.

Asset-based approaches begin with the sense that God does more than expect obedience to needs-fulfilling commands, but also permits believers to choose the best ways by which God's purpose can be enacted. Faith communities who use this approach experience a God who is always at work, always present, always powerful.

Maturing in an asset-based ministry creates happy, effective, engaged leadership. As this choice to be abundant takes hold, communities of faith will note that in their fellowship:

- Leaders are identified and equipped with vision and initiative.
- A broad sense of ownership and accountability develops.
- The ability to take risks for the sake of growth is born or develops.
- Decision making is simplified and based on permission-giving principles.
- A hopeful spirit grows.

The cardinal virtue here is summed up in the concept of utility. A simple phrase characterizes its meaning: "Use what you have to get what you want." For Christians, the phrase is adapted, *"Use what God has given you to get done what God wants."*

To easily begin using this process is to assay the congregation's assets as specifically as possible, knowing that in the naming of useful gifts each person will find a God-blessed utility that compels action on God's behalf and according to God's purpose. This personal reflection can be astonishingly joyful.

The classic way to understand the concept of asset-based approaches has been to characterize two points of view: one can look at a water glass as either half full or half empty. This can be oversimplified as being optimistic or pessimistic; actually it is a test of the observer's understanding of how useful the glass and its contents might be.

A lifetime of generosity is the natural response of every Christian to God's generous offering of love. The believer's life is marked with a continual giving away of God's blessings in order to extend God's sovereignty. Generosity is founded in gratitude and love. Christians are never really in the position of giving back to God because there is nothing we receive that has ever been ours in the first place. Instead, there is a free and willing response to what God has given with no sense of deserving. The church, as one of God's primary instruments in the world, serves as a storehouse with a gathering and concentrating purpose. Generosity is not just an attitude. Everything we have and are is for God's use. Our lives, we learn as disciples of Jesus Christ, are not our own.

In the Order of Meeting suggested for vestries (p. 82), the time begins with Bible study. Consider the following for use.

A biblical survey gives rich underpinnings to asset-based ministry. In any passage or story in which adversity is overcome, new life made possible, or God's purposes accomplished, look for evidence of the assets that were identified and put to use. For example, in Mark 6, the Feeding of Five Thousand, the problem of hungry people is obvious. But it might be easy to overlook the assets of that specific time and place, the readiness of people and Jesus' disciples to learn, even the unavailability of food in nearby towns. The small amounts of bread and fish certainly qualify as assets, too, and Jesus uses them all. (Other examples: The stories of Gideon, Samson, Deborah, and the guerrilla forces of David.)

Train your reading and hearing of the Scriptures so that you recognize "asset" words and phrases that might have otherwise gone unnoticed. For example, listen for what is useful in Titus 3:14, 2 Timothy 3:16, and 2 Peter 1:8.

In every story or passage, the basic question becomes, "What's helpful or useful here for understanding the nature of God, God's action, God's will?" "What or who is God using here, toward God's purposes?"

Although utility cannot be required as the core of every passage of the Scripture, see what happens when you use this lens through which to read familiar passages or stories. For example, look at the Beatitudes (Matt. 5:1–12). Might we see less about the deficits of neediness and more about the strength of blessings?

Read the passages that follow. Can you discern a biblical background for the philosophy and practice of asset-based ministry?

Psalm 34:8–9: In the most difficult of times, David can still say that "God's taste" reveals God's abundance. Verse 9 promises that nothing will be lacking for those who fear the Lord.

Matthew 10:5–15; Luke 10:1–12: We might fail to see in these "sending out" stories that Jesus exhibits full confidence that his followers have the capabilities to accomplish what he hopes.

Mark 16:14–18; Luke 24:36–49; John 20:19–23; and Acts 1:6–8: These readings about Jesus' ascension suggest that, in addition to the specific elements of The Great Commission, other possibilities and assets were also noted as worthy activities for Jesus' followers to pursue. This commission may derive its greatness, in fact, from its broad possibilities, not its specific command.

Mark 16:17a: If belief is an asset, then Jesus' words here give great hope to all believers. What we can accomplish in God's name comes back to the Spirit-graced gift of belief.

John 13:34b: Love is the primary ingredient of Christ's work on earth, and can be extended to others.

John 15:1–17; John 17; 1 Corinthians 12; and Ephesians 4: These texts illustrate how the binding together of the body of Christ into a community of believers knit tightly in common purpose is an asset of the whole that is always greater than its individual parts. Asset-based thinking is never individualistic.

2 Corinthians 12:8ff: Real or imagined weaknesses, even physical sufferings, are still assets, well within the power of God to use for God's purposes.

Ephesians 4:11–13: The purpose of church leaders is to equip saints for their ministries. "Building assets" might be another way of describing this compelling toward ministry in the world.

1 John 4:18a: The negativity of needs-based approaches is based on fears of all kinds. Perfect love negates fear.

How to Do Asset Mapping

Gather people in a room with sufficient tables and chairs for everyone. On each table provide pencils and pens and a quantity of sticky notes so that each person, including children, may write (or draw in the case of young children) at least twenty personal assets. An alternative to sticky notes is index cards; masking tape (not transparent tape) will also be needed.

When the people have gathered, it is helpful to set the context of abundance by a brief presentation using the concepts that precede this section. A brief Bible study may be included. Then ask everyone to write down twenty assets, gifts, or blessings that they are willing to share through God's church. Use the following to define and assist the process.

Post in large print or project on a screen these statements:

- an asset is a gift known for its usefulness
- five types of assets: individual, associations, institutions, physical, and economic
- assets include head, hands, and heart
- three asset-sparking questions: what are you good at doing? what do you like to do? what do you have that's useful?

Ask table groups to begin listing one asset, gift, talent, skill, or blessing on each note or card. Ask them to print and to put their name at the bottom. If children are present, use language that includes them. Suggest that they draw pictures to show what they can give.

During the process a leader can make suggestions. The leader can ask, "Who do you know? What is a dormant skill you have? What did you study in school? Does anyone owe you a favor you could call an asset?" If anyone is stuck, suggest they ask the table group for help or go to another table and see how others are getting in touch with their assets. Allow about twenty minutes for this.

When time has elapsed, ask participants to place the sticky notes indicating their assets randomly on a wall. If the sticky notes do not adhere well to the surface, put a large expanse of continuous-roll paper on the wall before the exercise. As the leader progresses to the next phase, do some multiplication. Multiply the number of people in the room by twenty. Tell everyone the number and that it indicates what richness God gives the church. Remember, everything posted on the wall is a given gift. No one has to be asked to give it; they are simply going to be invited to use it.

What happens next can take several directions. Invite groups to go to the wall and rearrange the assets into an affinity group. What ideas are generated by particular groupings? If a concept evolves, invite those whose gifts are represented in the grouping to pull together in the room and make a simple plan for implementation.

Another way to use the assets on the wall is to bring an idea to it. What are we going to do for formation in Lent? If you see such assets as woodworking, baking, love of children, play the piano, good at drawing, good organizer, what would you do with these assets in Lent? You could also "ask the wall" who would be good working with youth, teaching in church school, helping with financial affairs, leading a missional effort for students, or preparing church dinners.

Another approach is to use this process with a subgroup within the church.

It could be your outreach team, your casserole brigade for shut-ins, or parents of small children. The focus narrows and the asset mapping asks its questions within the context of the group. Participants are asked for assets that specifically relate to food, or children, or outreach. Be sure to encourage connections that might stretch the imagination. Ask for a smaller number of assets, perhaps ten per participant.

Promise everyone who offers their assets for use in the church and the world that at least one of their assets will be called upon within six months (preferably three months). The leadership team should adopt a process that ensures this promise is kept. As well, using the wall, find someone good at organizing to sort all the assets into a useable format (paper or computer). They will likely need help in this collation; consult the wall again for additional help.

Celebrate the gifts. Find a way to incorporate their use in your liturgy, perhaps by offering the gifts to be blessed.

Repeat the process at least annually and use the small group version as needed.

The Five Marks of Mission

According to Presiding Bishop Katharine Jefferts Schori, "Mission is what we are sent out to do. Mission is reconciling the world to God and each other in Christ, according to the Book of Common Prayer. In Jesus' terms, mission is both caring for 'the least of these' as he talks about Matthew 25 (we might also use the phrase 'preferential option for the poor'), and going into the world, baptizing, and teaching others about Jesus' work, as he elucidates in Matthew 28."[79] The Presiding Bishop went on to describe the Five Marks of Mission and the church's engagement with them.

The Five Marks of Mission were offered to the church by the Anglican Consultative Council in 1984 and affirmed by bishops of the Anglican Communion at the Lambeth Conferences in 1988 and 1998. The Episcopal Church affirmed the Five Marks of Mission in 2009 through a resolution of the General Convention. The marks enable Christians to have a common focus as they share in God's mission in the world.

Five Marks of Mission

1. To proclaim the good news of the Kingdom

Proclamation needs to be not only in words—effective communication of the gospel—but also in actions, by living the Good News we preach (Exod. 3; Isa. 61:1–3; Mark 1:1–8; Luke 9:1–6; John 13:1–17; Acts 8:25–40).

---

79. Presiding Bishop Katharine Jefferts Schori to the Executive Council on October 21, 2011. Accessed online at www.episcopalchurch.org/newsline_130289_ENG_HTM.htm on December 18, 2011.

2. To teach, baptize, and nurture new believers

Christian discipleship is about lifelong learning. We all need formal and informal resources for growing in faith, so that the church is a learning environment for all ages (Deut. 6:1–9; Neh. 8:1–18; Titus 2; Acts 19:1–10; John 3:1–15; Luke 24:13–35).

3. To respond to human need by loving service

Churches have a long tradition of care through pastoral and social ministry. Christians are called to respond to the needs of people locally and in the wider human community (2 Kings 5:1–14; Job 2:11–13; Heb. 13:1–6; 1 Pet. 5:1–7; Matt. 25:31–46; John 4:1–30).

4. To seek to transform unjust structures in society

Jesus, and the Old Testament prophets before him, challenged oppressive structures in God's name. Christians are called not only to press for change, but also to demonstrate justice within church structures (Exod. 23:1–13; Amos 2:4–16; James 2:14–26; Matt. 23:23–36; Mark 10:13–27; Luke 19:1–10).

5. To strive to safeguard the integrity of creation, and sustain and renew the life of the earth

The Bible's vision of salvation is universal in its scope. We are called to promote the well-being of the human community and its environment, so that Creation may live in harmony (Deut. 26; Ps. 65; Rom. 8:18–25; Rev. 22:1–5; Matt. 6:25–31; Mark 6:30–52).

"Mission goes out from God. Mission is God's way of loving and saving the world . . . So mission is never our invention or choice."[80] The initiative is always God's, not ours. Believers are called and equipped in baptism to serve God's mission by living and proclaiming the Good News.

> Draw your church together, O Lord, into one great company of disciples, together following our Lord Jesus Christ into every walk of life, together serving him in his mission to the world, and together witnessing to his love on every continent and island. We ask this in His name and for His sake. Amen.

Using the Marks of Mission

With a vestry or any leadership group, consider these questions in relationship to each Mark of Mission. These questions would work well in the Mission time in the Order of Meeting (agenda) of a vestry meeting. The biblical citations might also be used for Bible study using the methods found in this resource section.

---

80. The Lambeth Conference 1998, Section II, p. 121.

Present each Mark of Mission and ask:

• What is it in the life of our congregation that shows that this Mark of Mission matters to us?

• How do we see this Mark of Mission in our worship? Our fellowship? Our teaching?

• What further could be undertaken to show that this Mark of Mission is alive and engaged in our congregation?

• Who else in our community outside our congregation does this? How can we support them? How can we cooperate with them?

The Story We Tell and the Story God Tells

What and who forms the story of your congregation? Has the corporate memory been recorded in a book? Are there matriarchs or patriarchs who can tell the tales of yore? Young churches have stories too. Though shorter, these stories of founding the church will have their own constitutive power. Listen to, read, or recall the story of your congregation, especially the way it has been led. Note the major themes.

When you collect these themes, you will be creating an *ecclesiology* [*ecclesia* = church as body of believers or building + *ology* = study of]. This study of your congregation will indicate what you value, what principles were/are formative, and a future trajectory. The honest narrative will find components that bind and restrict and others that free and release the people for participation in the larger narrative of the "one, holy, catholic, and apostolic church."

All our speaking, doing, and thinking is the stuff out of which the story is created and shaped. Keen observers of the life of the church in all its manifestations (local, regional, national, global, and universal) can deduce varying and sometimes competing stories or ecclesiologies. As the narrative radiates out beyond the local congregation, the local story is embedded in, reoriented, corrected, and expanded by larger narratives. The specific images of the congregation are comingled with our salvation history in the Scriptures, the sacramental life of the church, its creeds, teaching, and authority structures. This larger narrative serves to keep local expressions of church rightly ordered. The more local expressions of church remind us that regional and national bodies of the church are to be grounded, realistic, and missionally engaged.

Our congregational stories may be about the earliest days of providing "mission schools" to educate children before the availability of public education or building the first hospital in the community. They may be about the decades of influence of a patriarch or matriarch. They may be about lean times or glory days, scarcity or abundance. These stories contribute to the human quest of making sense of the environments we inhabit. And the healthiest stories tell of how a particular gathering of the faithful is living into God's future under the guidance of the Holy Spirit.

When story is broadened to include a larger context, the content shifts as well. Dioceses tell stories of liturgical styles and capital fund drives. National churches recall prayer book revisions, missionary endeavors, or controversial decisions. At the level of the Anglican Communion, markers of our shared ecclesiology are debated, declared, and ultimately received as consonant with teaching of the "one, holy, catholic, and apostolic church."

A Larger Narrative

For Episcopalians, the pieces of our communion's story—an Anglican ecclesiology—include being a part of the Church Catholic, having the historic episcopate, adhering to the ancient creeds, believing that the Scriptures declare all things necessary to salvation, and observing the sacraments of baptism and the Holy Eucharist.[81] Anglicans would also describe their particular nuanced ecclesiology as including a deep yearning for unity and comprehension, an appeal to the teachings of the early Church while also appreciating contemporary scholarship, love of the doctrine of the incarnation (God *being made flesh* in Jesus Christ), and the beloved theological rationale of *lex orendi, lex credendi* ("the law of prayer is the law of belief," "we pray our beliefs," "what we pray is what we believe").[82]

How we conceive of and talk about the church extends both influence and formative power over how we speak about the nature of God, how we structure our life together, and how we together live the divine call and invitation to participate in God's mission in the world. In the last few decades there has been an enrichment of the story of how we are constituted as the people of God, the church.

---

81. The last four markers are those of the "Chicago-Lambeth Quadrilateral."

82. To dig a little deeper and to be pointed even more deeply, read Bishop Pierre Whalon's "Peering Past Lambeth" at Anglicans Online: http://anglicansonline.org/resources/essays/whalon/PeeringPastLambeth.html

The Grand Narrative

The Holy Trinity has been foundational as an organizing concept for mission. Specifically, the New Testament concept of koinonia (community, communion, fellowship) is observed in the definitive nature of the persons of the Trinity. "This fresh reconsideration of trinitarian theology gives us a vision of God as a dynamic community of mutuality, openness, difference, and love that makes space for others to participate. These qualities define the image of God in which we are created. One of the major paradigm shifts to come from this focus on a relational Trinity is the shift from an image of God (*imago Dei*) conception based on isolated individuals, to a relational, communal view. . . . "[83]

The essential nature of God is found in the Holy Trinity. The essential missional nature of the church, consequently, is rooted in the relational and communal nature of God rather than in hierarchically, bureaucratically, or individualistically created human structures. The Triune God is a communion[84] of generative love that overflows into every crevice of the created order. In the character of every ecclesial community is found its identity through God's saving activity through the freeing, justifying work of Christ sustained by the Holy Spirit. This formation moves the people of God toward a right relationship with God, the natural order, and with all humanity.

The context of this movement is the reign of God. Humans experience this as God's redemptive presence in the world. The sending of the Holy Spirit, celebrated as Pentecost and called the birthday of the church, embeds that same action—sending—in the constitution of the church. Mission, therefore, becomes not just a program or activity of the church as the people of God, but the essential purpose of the church. The reign of God is the sign of the present reality and the foretaste of what is to come: the restoration of unity between God and humanity. The story God tells is that God is for us and has created an instrument—the church—to tell and live the story. The story we tell is how we participate in that redemptive saga.

> Mission is the creating, reconciling and transforming action of God, flowing from the community of love found in the Trinity, made known to all humanity in the person of Jesus, and entrusted to the faithful action and witness of the people of God who, in the power of the Spirit, are a sign, foretaste and instrument of the reign of God.
>
> —National Council of Churches in Australia

---

83. Craig Van Gelder and Dwight J. Zscheile, *The Missional Church in Perspective* (Grand Rapids, MI: Baker Academic, 2011), Kindle edition, 108.

84. See Van Gelder and Zscheile, *Missional Church in Perspective*, 54–55, 105–110 for a discussion of *perichoresis* (communal and mutual indwelling nature of God).

Leadership and Pentecost

This essay began with a question of how God's sons and daughters in congregations, acting individually and collectively, have shaped their story. We next turned to the larger theological consideration of how God continues to speak into the church (locally and universally) and how this reflection on the nature of the church has been extended through a refreshed understanding of the Holy Trinity. For leaders in the church, this consideration of the Trinity has implications. "The Triune God is always seeking to invite and draw all creation into the reconciled communion of the divine life. That is the ultimate destiny of the church and indeed the cosmos. As such, it is the ultimate end or *telos* of Christian leadership."[85]

The Feast of Pentecost[86] celebrates the outpouring of the Spirit intended to lead the community into truth. Those who experienced this pyrotechnic moment in the life of the fledgling church were its leaders. What is worth noting?

The first thing is that that those leaders were energized. Stressed and fractured leaders found the "power from on high" to speak a common language declaring what truly and deeply matters to every human being. The crucifixion of Christ is certainly an experience that would deplete any follower. These leaders found the graced ability to take the deepest human discouragement, place it in a greater story of significance, and invite hearers into new vitality and purpose.

Second, the language of Pentecost transcended distinctions and differences, tribe and culture. Having read more of the story in Scripture and in church history, we know that there are continual challenges to this unity. It is leaders,[87] energized by the Holy Spirit, who aid in the discernment of a common way forward in mission. Leaders were enabled to speak across cultural boundaries and unify the community in its new reality where there is "no longer Jew or Greek, there is no longer slave or free, there is no longer male or female" (Gal. 3:28).

Third, the effect of being led into truth is that leaders were equipped with the capacity to help the church make sense out of the experience of Jesus among them and begin to answer the question, "Now what?" The response to that question is still underway among the people of God and the Spirit's

---

85. Dwight J. Zscheile, "The Trinity, Leadership, and Power," *Journal of Religious Leadership* 6, no. 2 (Fall 2007): 52.

86. Interestingly, in the Eastern Church, Pentecost is a three-day festival and the Sunday of the festival is known as "Trinity Sunday." Western Christians keep a Trinity Sunday one week after the celebration of the Day of Pentecost.

87. See Acts 15 for an early story of this discernment.

presence is still needed. Leaders in all Christian communities help discern what God is doing today and invite their sisters and brothers to join that activity. An essential role of the leader is to live in the midst of the cacophony of sounds and messages. Using the biblical witness, the divine action in the tradition and history of the church, and God-given reason, leaders sort out that which is not true from the Truth. Then an invitation is offered to the faithful to join God's vision for mission in the community.

Leaders listen, first and foremost, to the story in and among the community of the faithful and its connection to the Big Story. God's future is then discerned through a lens that is experienced as trustworthy, nonauthoritarian, culture transcending, and energizing. God's future is mission and all the baptized have an essential role in this unfolding story.

RESOURCE H
A Primer on Permission-Giving Churches

There is a constellation of practices that support an appreciative or asset-based approach to living in the church, the body of Christ. The truth pointed to in being a permission-giving church is found in the work of William Easum in his book *Sacred Cows Make Gourmet Burgers.*[88] The premise is that the church's passion should be to make disciples, not managerial decisions. A permission-giving church lives to say *yes* instead of *no.*

The fear that exists in many congregations is that if someone (or some group) is not guarding the permission granting, bad things will happen. There are those who would rather that a church stagnate and die than let it run the risk of making a mistake. Fear of failure is endemic in American culture. The alternative is to allow something new to happen that may thrive and, perhaps, commit some mistakes along the way. Mistakes are best seen as learning experiences, not as fatal or terminal.

Permission-giving churches work always to err on the side of giving permission to new ministries. They are, in a default setting, on the side of the implementation of new ministries through a ministry team, composed of people who have a vested interest in the success of a particular ministry.

Trust and love are at the heart of permission-giving churches. Love lets go and permits everyone to stretch his or her wings. Trust allows members to step into new, perhaps uncharted, territory with confidence. Actually, trust operates on mutual respect. Grace abounds in permission-giving churches. Permission-giving churches encourage every member, not just a select few, to

---

88. William M. Easum, *Sacred Cows Make Gourmet Burgers* (Nashville: Abingdon Press, 1995).

live out their spiritual gifts by either joining or starting a small group effort, ministry team, or mission thrust.

In churches that have permission giving as a principle, people exercise their spiritual gifts because they want to, because they receive incredible amounts of fulfillment; the parish includes people who are equipped to use their spiritual gifts and don't burn out easily or become demoralized, because they are so energized by using those gifts.

There is encouragement for people who engage in ministry to make as many of the decisions as possible about how to carry out the ministry. Pushing decision making to the level closest to the people who will engage the mission or ministry is an example of subsidiarity (see "The Principle of Subsidiarity" on page 91).

Are boundaries and accountability needed? Of course. Those who use their God-given permission to create mission and ministry efforts get their guidance and accountability from the church's lived core values, not from confusing accountability with control. Control is deciding what people can and can't do; accountability is rendering an account of what a person has or has not already done. Those who take this kind of permission will be happy to give an account of the place God has taken them.

Permission-giving churches help people grow spiritually rather than simply getting them involved in activities. They encourage each person to look within, to discover his or her gifts, for the purpose of sharing those gifts with the body of Christ. This experience of permission giving creates an open environment in which all the people are encouraged and equipped to do extraordinary ministry. Churches with this positive, unlocked attitude develop and articulate the mission and vision of the church and create the environment in which people are free to live out their spiritual gifts without having to navigate through an elaborate (and sometimes negative) institutional bureaucracy.

> Permission-giving churches experience the grace of God to encourage, empower, and equip the people of God to use their God-given talents to share the gospel and participate in the Reign of God.

As William Easum wrote, "Permission-giving churches require a new mind-set that is comfortable with the fundamental paradox of the Quantum Age—loosely knit networks and high levels of synergy. Networks and synergy are accomplished because each congregation is clear about its values and mission, and also gives permission for each person to live out those values and mission through the exercise of their spiritual gifts."[89]

There are several key principles that are honored by permission-giving churches:

---

89. William M. Easum, *Sacred Cows Make Gourmet Burgers*, 55.

- The people of God have permission to be God's agents and missionaries in the world every hour, every day, every week, as they bring their gifts to bear on those whom they meet in the world.

- Leaders are secure enough to equip others for ministry and get out of the way and let them develop their ministries.

- Ministry and mission may be delivered at any time, in any place, by anyone to discern God's reign for any person or circumstance in need.

- Those who exercise this permission are happy to be accountable for the ministry they undertake through their baptismal vows.

- Congregations that are permission giving develop flat organizational structures that encourage and facilitate ministry rather than managing or coordinating it.

In permission-giving churches, the grace of God and the ministry of all the baptized thrives.

Creating a Vestry Covenant

This source also available online.

Gathering Principles and Building a Covenant

In chapter 7, the practice of establishing a vestry covenant is presented. No covenant is created out of nothing. There is much of a parish's life together that must be sorted through and new practices that must be tested to create a list of principles for possible inclusion in a vestry covenant. Build a list of principles by taking note of what you uncover in the life of the parish. Use your Leadership School time to start this collection early in the vestry year. The minutes of the meeting are a good place to archive your discoveries. An example of a principle in your parish may be your provision of rich worship, or lively formation for children or adults, your long-standing commitment to collegial decision making through consensus, or your commitment to engaging God's mission in your neighborhood.

Another source of additions to the list of principles you honor will be this book and others like it. From these pages select those principles that will be most helpful and sustaining or that will create a healthy climate among the baptized people of God who gather as your community of faith. Consider seriously naming the offering of anonymous information and communication triangles as practices that will no longer have a place in your life together. Remember, when you deny someone a favored and fallen communication path, an alternative, healthy way must be offered in its place.

Writing the Covenant

After a process of discernment, the vestry names the key principles that are significant for them in their life together. This is done in a brainstorming or "popcorn" method: members simply name out loud those points that are vital, and a recorder writes them on a piece of newsprint. Make sure to introduce the principles you have noted in the vestry meeting leading up to this point.

A leader in this covenant-writing process helps focus on that which is significant. This focus ensures that the full spectrum of congregational ministry—within and outside the parish—is represented in the covenant. After recording the values and principles, group and rename them if necessary.

When you have a final list of key points, ask the group as a whole or a writing team to place these points into a paragraph. The charge to this team is to build a statement that is both complete *and* succinct. This is a challenge. Upon completion, read the statement and make any necessary refinements. Then ask all present to sign it.

The vestry places this vestry covenant in a prominent place in the church and parishioners are invited to endorse the covenant by signing it too. Presenting the covenant to the parish creates broader ownership and gives the parish information on the vestry's operational principles.

There is an extension to the use of a vestry covenant that your church may find helpful. Give each ministry team or group in the parish (choir, outreach, education, and so on) a copy of the vestry covenant. Ask them to adopt the covenant as a preamble (perhaps slightly reworded to fit the circumstance) to a covenant they write for their team. Their process would mirror the vestry's process. Any member of the vestry could coach a group that desires to adopt a covenant.

A brief liturgy recognizing this work should mark the document's creation. Consider having it presented and read during the Eucharist and blessed at the altar.

Covenants should be renewed annually and refreshed or rewritten at least every three years.

Bible Study

This source also available online.

Lectio Divina

For centuries—probably dating back to the twelfth century—Christians have practiced a unique form of biblical study and reflection known as *lectio divina* (divine reading). This technique is a slow, contemplative reading of Scripture that allows the individual or group to come into union with God. As we move deeply into the study/prayer of the Word of God "with the ear of our hearts,"[90] we are tuned to the ways of God, discovering the rhythm of the movement of the Holy Spirit. This discovery builds the ability to offer ourselves in mission.

The first step is reading or listening (*lectio*) to the Scripture, slowly and purposefully. The intent in this stage is to listen for the voice of God to speak personally, pressing to hear the phrase or word God is offering for the day. Upon finding the word or phrase, meditation (*meditatio*), the second step, begins. The practitioner follows the example of Mary "pondering in her heart" the news of Jesus' birth by letting the given word or phrase interact with our thinking and feeling at our deepest level. Prayer (*oratio*) is the third movement. In this step the presence of the living God is sought conversationally (silently or aloud). The final movement is resting in the presence of God, the one who invites us into God's transformative, loving embrace. In this step, called contemplation (*contemplatio*), words are unnecessary.

Lectio divina is a spiritual practice. It is an inward activity, not an outward one, taking the student to the depths of the human encounter with the God of transformation. We may begin with doing an exercise, but as we arrive in the fourth movement of contemplation, we have arrived at a place of being. This resting in the Presence grounds and sustains our identity as God's sons and daughters.

---

90. Prologue to the Rule of Saint Benedict.

Solitary Use of *Lectio Divina*

Choose a biblical text that you wish to read/pray. The daily lectionary is a good source for ideas. God will lead to an alternative, if needful. Locate a place of comfort and quiet. Begin with a time of centering and then read the text slowly. God will give you a word or phrase upon which to focus. Meditate upon the word or phrase. Then speak to God in prayer. Finally, rest in God's love. This private form is the traditional use *of lectio divina.*

Group Use of *Lectio Divina*

There has grown up a corporate use of the practice of *lectio divina* in the last few decades. This method uses a facilitator. The text is read three times, each time by a different person. The reading is followed by silence. During the first reading, a word or phrase comes to rest in the heart of the hearer. After the silence, just that word or phrase is shared. The second reading is offered as the hearers "hear" or "see" Christ in the text and how he is touching their life that day. This experience of Christ is shared after the silence. The third reading is a "calling forth" listening. After the silence following the reading, hearers share what they believe they are being called to do or become. The exercise is concluded by each person praying for the person on their right.

Lectio divina, an ancient spiritual practice, teaches us about the God who loves us and consecrates our life and times in the service of that love. We learn who we are at the deepest levels of our lives—members of the household of God.

African Bible Study

The African Bible Study method is intended to create space to hear the voice of God. Any Scripture may be the subject of study. As God speaks and direction is perceived, participants discern what God is calling them to be and sending them to do. In a group context, the discernment is mutually edifying and encouraging. Here are the steps:

- Open with simple prayer.
- Ask everyone to *listen for a word or phrase that catches his or her attention.*
- Read the selected text.
- Ask each participant to share their word or phrase. Discussion may follow the sharing.
- Suggest that everyone consider *where the text touches his or her life* before the reading of the passage a second time by another person.
- Give participants a chance to share their reflections; discussion may follow.

- Present the third direction for reflection: *"How is God calling me to respond?"*
- Another person reads the text a third time.
- Give each person time to share his or her reflection and allow for group discussion to follow.
- Close with prayer so that intentions may be lifted to God.

The African Bible Study method requires no special theological skills. It honors the truth that all the baptized have access to the wisdom and guidance of God. Allow everyone to participate at a level that is appropriate and comfortable; anyone may pass at any time. Active, nonjudgmental listening is expected. As well, we are not present to solve problems for anyone else. The flow of the study allows for a godly oscillation between what is being heard deep within and what is happening in our engagement with the world.

Dwelling in the Word[91]

This method spends half an hour or more dwelling within a particular biblical passage. Any passage or the daily lectionary may be used. The invitation is for the text to expand thinking, open new pathways, encourage creativity, and make way for the Holy Spirit. A passage may be dwelt upon for weeks and months.

Here is the method. Begin with prayer. Choose a text and read it. Sit together with the passage, in silence and in conversation. After considering these missional questions, close with prayer.

- What did you notice as you read the passage?
- What is the context, based on what the passage says? How is that like or unlike the way we live today?
- What is God doing in this passage? What is God doing here and now that is similar?
- How is God sending you in this passage? How is the church being sent in this passage?

---

91. See a variation on Dwelling in the Word in Alan Roxburgh's *Practicing Hospitality—The Workbook* from Missional Network, available for download at www.roxburghmissionalnet .com.

Gospel Based Discipleship

from the Native American *A Disciple's Prayer Book*[92]

- The Gathering Prayer (unison)

  Creator, we give you thanks for all you are and all you bring to us for our visit within your creation. In Jesus, you place the Gospel in the center of this sacred circle through which all of creation is related. You show us the way to live a generous and compassionate life. Give us your strength to live together with respect and commitment as we grow in your spirit, for you are God, now and forever. Amen.

- The Gathering Psalm of Praise *from Lectionary or a canticle from the Daily Office*

- Gospel of the Day *from the Lectionary*

- Response: *Reflect and Respond to the Gospel of the Day*

  What word(s), idea(s), or sentence(s) stand out for you in the Gospel of the Day? (Reread the Gospel.)

  What is Jesus (the Gospel) saying to you ? (Reread the Gospel.)

  What is Jesus (the Gospel) calling you to do?

- Apostles' Creed

  I believe in God, the Father almighty, creator of heaven and earth.

  I believe in Jesus Christ, God's only Son, our Lord.

  who was conceived by the Holy Spirit and born of the Virgin Mary, suffered under Pontius Pilate, was crucified, died, and was buried;

  he descended to the dead. On the third day he rose again;

  he ascended into heaven, he is seated at the right hand of the Father, and he will come again to judge the living and the dead. I believe in the Holy Spirit, the holy catholic Church,

  the communion of saints, the forgiveness of sins,

  the resurrection of the body, and the life everlasting. Amen.
- Prayers

  Individual and Group Prayers of **A**doration, **C**onfession, **T**hanksgiving, **S**upplication (ACTS)

- Collects *from the Daily Office or other sources*

---

92. "A Disciple's Prayer Book" Native American Ministries, Episcopal Church Center, 1999. This booklet is out of print. A PDF is available at http://archive.episcopalchurch.org/documents/NAM_a_disciples_prayer_book.pdf. The PDF version uses of above outline within the context of each season of the Church Year.

•The Lord's Prayer

on occasion a Rule of Life is recited:
> Creator God we acknowledge and give thanks that:
> In Jesus we know we belong to a Sacred Circle
>> with the Gospel and Baptismal Covenant in the Center.
> In this Sacred Circle:
>> We are all related;
>> We life a compassionate and generous life;
>> We respect all life, traditions, and resources;
>> We commit ourselves to spiritual growth, discipleship
>> and consensus.

Please note: Inductive Bible Study must always be a component of a larger context of practicing the faith. That larger dimension is the corporate nature of our faith. As we move within all the modes (individual, household, small group, larger community) of our lives as disciples of Christ, the mutually interdependent nature of that experience both informs and corrects us in our hearing and service.

Using an Action-Reflection Model

This source also available online.

In the last half of the twentieth century, variants on the action-reflection model of learning multiplied. The model's use became common in seminaries and popularized in the church through the adult learning program known as Education for Ministry (EfM) from the School of Theology at the University of the South. This process is, in a secular environment, the ability to reflect on one's actions so that continuous learning occurs. When this disciplined capacity to pay attention to everyday action and activity is then placed under the lens of values and principles, developmental insight is the result.

Here is a visual overview of theological action-reflection:

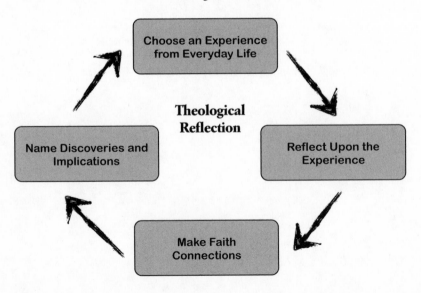

When used in the church, the story of God and God's relationship with the world and its people become the lens employed for reflection. When used in this specific way, the process is generally referred to as theological reflection, with theology understood in its focusing on God's activity in human life. Use of an action-reflection model can be a significant incubator for both the formation of leaders and the claiming of the mission that God holds for every community of faith.

Here is a process any group may use. While designed for individual use, it may easily be adapted for the vestry or leadership group to reflect on a communal experience. This particular method, from Abigail Johnson's book, *Reflecting with God: Connecting Faith and Daily Life in Small Groups*,[93] amplifies the four core parts into six elements:

1. Choosing an Experience: name an event on which to reflect

Choose an event, a moment, a conversation, or a situation. As you recall the event, ask:

- What happened?
- Who was involved?
- What was said or done?

2. Exploring the Experience: finding another layer to the event

To explore another layer in this event, ask yourself:

- How did you feel?
- What challenged, stimulated, or disturbed you?
- What was happening for others in the situation?

3. Digging Deeper: expanding your thinking

To discover another layer of reflection, ask yourself:

- What do you think about the situation?
- What core values emerge as you think about this event?
- What values are different from yours?
- What social issues, power issues, or economic issues are at work?

---

93. Abigail Johnson, *Reflecting with God: Connecting Faith and Daily Life in Small Groups* (Herndon, VA: Alban Institute, 2004). Permission sought.

4. Making Faith Connections: finding God at work in this event

To make faith connections, ask:

- Where is God present for you in this situation?
- Where is God present for others?
- Does this event remind you of a Scripture passage, a hymn, or other resource from your faith tradition?
- What theological issues or themes are present?
- What traditions of our church speak to this situation?
- Are you affirmed or challenged in your present actions or beliefs?

5. Learning: naming your discoveries

To draw out what you learned, ask:

- What questions still linger?
- Were you challenged to change present actions or beliefs?
- What have you learned about yourself?
- What have you learned about God?
- What do you need?
- What will you do now?

6. Praying: taking time with God

Conclude the reflection with prayer.

Using a theological action-reflection process is not easy in the beginning. Developing skills and comfort with the process takes time and experience. The benefit is to have a practice that provides everyone in the group a disciplined way to apply faith to life and imagine implications for a useful and faithful outcome. While a theological action-reflection usually begins with an individual, it should always move to a universal level, allowing everyone opportunity for growth through the reflection.

If the discussion/decision making in the action-reflection model gets bogged down, take time out to process an issue theologically. This will likely push the normal time parameter over the limit but the investment will be worth it.

Navigating
Church Conflict

Christ Church is located in an idyllic setting. Just off the town square, it has impressive stone walls punctuated by stained glass. Presiding over the beautifully kept grounds is a tall tower with a large cross. The town has grown in the last decades into a small city.

Christ Church has a relatively new rector who came to the parish right out of seminary. When he surveyed his new church, he noted that the congregation was substantially gray with a few households made up of younger generational cohorts. So small in number were those young parishioners in the congregation that the church used mostly adult acolytes. No Sunday school was held. There was a healing service and Bible study midweek. About a hundred souls occupied the pews on Sunday. Two decades ago, two hundred worshipped on a typical Sunday. The vestry was composed of the majority age group and most members had served on the vestry many years. A long-serving finance committee regularly met with the vestry to manage their dwindling resources.

Upon returning from a conference, the rector and two parishioners, one of whom was on the vestry and the other the parent of two teenagers, were convinced that a shift was necessary for the church to remain viable. The focus of the conference was a presentation on the dramatic reordering of the church's place in culture and a celebration of the church's return to its core value in the Great Commission to be missional by making disciples and serving its community.

The three presented an idea to the vestry about a way to begin community engagement. What they had conceived on the ride home was a tutoring center that would be allied with the poorest performing public school in the county, a school located directly behind their church. They did not expect the responses they got.

The first voices to speak came from the finance committee: "We have no extra funds at all. It is enormously expensive to keep these historic buildings in order and we already have too much deferred maintenance." Another chimed in, "What will it mean for us to have all these children running around our parish hall? Remember when the last rector wanted to have a soup kitchen here?" Another spoke, "I bet our liability insurance would go through the roof." And another asked, "Where would we get tutors to do this?"

The three spoke of the Great Commandment, of the missional use of their buildings, of the twelve retired teachers and one school superintendent in the congregation. Several on the vestry seemed to warm to the idea and spoke of the importance of the church to respond positively to the changes their church and most legacy churches were experiencing. But no decision could be made. There was no consensus.

After the meeting, the finance committee gathered in the hallway to continue the discussion. There was a similar little huddle of a few in the parking lot. The three who came with the idea were deflated. And, of course, e-mails flew as soon as some folks could get to their computers.

What would happen next?

Sources of Conflict[94]

1. The problem is not the problem. Everyone who is part of a conflict believes that they know who or what the problem is. It is highly unlikely that any one person has a complete view of what is happening. If you deal only with the issues on the surface, there will be no resolution. Every individual has his or her own set of filters and perceptions. From these perceptions we build a unique personal construct through which we view our world. This also means we can look at the same information and see it differently, thus creating a source of potential conflict.

Miscommunication is likely since we all have varying ways of interpreting. We send and receive information in unique ways. Conflict is a likely outcome of failed or misunderstood communication.

When attempting to achieve a particular end, we use power. It can be a force for good, if used in an appropriate way, or it can be a force that may try to coerce or manipulate. The fallen use of power generally tries to control what are perceived as scarce resources or to influence the way others behave.

A positive utilization of conflict is an understanding of power as an abundant resource rather than a scarce commodity. Healthy power is found not by dominating others, but rather by allowing everyone to fulfill their richest possibility and God-given potential within the community.

---

94. This discussion is based on the work of Donald Bussart in his essay "Growing Through Conflict," published by Iliff School of Theology, 1995.

2. **I am the source of most conflict I experience**. Used for selfish ends, power represents our attempt to force our needs and values on others. Often, our own needs and values are conflicted within us. In discourse with others, we may be attempting to resolve our own inner conflicts. There are three kinds of conflict: internal, interpersonal, and, collectively, within groups. The psychological dynamic is that we seek equilibrium between our inner and outer states. Conflict is a product of this dynamic. When we handle our inner and/or outer conflict poorly, our self-worth is damaged and becomes fragile.

> Everything that irritates us about others can lead us to an understanding of ourselves.
>
> —Carl Jung

What the church can offer in the midst of conflict is a positive, nonthreatening space of support and acceptance. When freedom is a value, openness and receptivity to others becomes possible. In a no-lose environment the goals of the self and the goals of others become compatible.

The Dynamics of Conflict

Though most consider conflict something to be avoided, this is not necessarily the case. The real issue is how we handle conflict. Dealing with it superficially will not work. Keeping the peace and denial will not work. Calling for a vote to polarize the group will not work. Effective use of conflict has a way of surfacing deeper issues and feelings so that there is a chance for resolution.

Destructive conflict is built of misperception, competition, anonymous information, triangular communication, threats, lack of transparency, and fallen expressions of power. Constructive conflict uses trust, openness, cooperation, openness to change and learning, cooperation, and an absence of threats or power plays.

The work of everyone in the midst of conflict is to move it to a constructive place where transformation can occur. Otherwise, things will spiral downward until a stasis (not a resolution) is achieved. Then the next time there is conflict, all the unresolved underlying issues will resurface in the guise of a new issue.

How to Turn Bad Conflict into Good

When there is intractable conflict in the church, help from the outside is required. When conflict happens in groups of relatively healthy people, resolution is likely. All leaders should be advocates of fair fighting, constructive conflict, and win-win attitudes.

Fair fighting includes observing and keeping some ground rules:

• mutual respect
• honoring the group's interdependence and mutual interests

- commitment to active listening to others
- not introducing anonymous information
- staying out of communication triangles
- not blaming, interrupting, or labeling
- not personalizing issues
- speaking only for yourself

Supportive and caring relationships are the positive ground in which resolution will grow. This does not imply lockstep unanimity. There is room for diversity and alternative opinions. The movement, however, for conflict resolution must be toward collaboration and acceptance of the richness that diversity can bring.

Constructive conflict grows out of a desire to integrate each other's personal goals with the best interests of everyone in mind. If the fight becomes seeking a solution that meets as many different needs as possible (instead of seeking a specific position or solution), conflict can be resolved.

A win-win resolution, while difficult to achieve, allows everyone to benefit. *Robert's Rules of Order* or canon law do not provide for this type of solution. The work is to create a common place upon which all (or at least most) can stand. When a great majority finds a common place to stand, the effort at conciliation should be considered a win. Even in the church, there are curmudgeons and contrarians.

Every time a conflict works its way to a godly resolution, a stronger, healthier foundation is built under the people of God. Unresolved conflict diminishes the present health of the church.

Conflict is a process. It is what lies between disruption and chaos in the past and what is harmonious and faithful in the future. This "between time" is the content of our Christian story. The old disruptive and diseased ways of relating to God were challenged in the faith saga. The conflict is seen in the cross; the reconciled, graced way of living with God is offered through Christ's triumph over the cross.

What happened at Christ Church? The story is actually a conflation of several incidents in three churches. In one case, a diocesan staff member helped the vestry work toward resolution. In another, the rector and senior warden were conflict-resolution savvy and helped the church leaders move its conflict to a healthy discussion and a place where all could stand. In the third, the conflict submerged and gets resurfaced regularly; there was no resolution.

The good news is that stuck is not a place we have to live.

Competencies Self-Assessment

This source also available online.

from chapter 10

SERVANT
concern for others' well-being
helps unleash gifts of others
serves as a hopeful companion

RELATIONAL
provides environment for hope & grace
concern for the team
builds relationships

EQUIPPING
affirms and acknowledges others
wise use of questions
encourages others to lifelong learning

NAVIGATIONAL
urges beyond stuck places
planning skills
points to safe passage

SELF-AWARENESS
balance and humility
nonanxious
ability to pay attention

FOCUS
can see rightly
offers insight & correction
helps people move forward

The center of the hexagon has a value of one and the outer edge a value of ten. Place a line parallel to the outer edge relative to the values of one to ten. One indicates that you have limited capacity in that category; ten equals great capacity. The closer your line is to the outer line, the higher you value your competency.

Consider sharing your results with fellow members of the vestry. Each person will have unique strengths to offer in leadership. Knowing each other's strengths will provide a leader or "go to" person for various ministries.

Reflect on your self-assessment. What might you do to enhance those areas which you noted as limited? Pay attention to your strengths. Where might they be used in your capacity as a leader?

Introduction to Servant Leadership

Robert Greenleaf, the founder of the modern servant-leadership movement, wrote:

> The servant-leader is servant first. . . . It begins with the natural feeling that one wants to serve, to serve first. Then conscious choice brings one to aspire to lead. That person is sharply different from one who is leader first, perhaps because of the need to assuage an unusual power drive or to acquire material possessions. . . The leader-first and the servant-first are two extreme types. Between them there are shadings and blends that are part of the infinite variety of human nature.
>
> The difference manifests itself in the care taken by the servant-first to make sure that other people's highest priority needs are being served. The best test, and difficult to administer, is: Do those served grow as persons? Do they, while being served, become healthier, wiser, freer, more autonomous, more likely themselves to become servants? And, what is the effect on the least privileged in society? Will they benefit or at least not be further deprived?[95]

The context for all leadership is relationships. It is a special form of relationship. In essence, servant leadership is about a choice people make to live in a particular relationship marked by mutual submission, caring interactions, and taking on roles that do not create a superior-inferior relationship. Through this unique way of organizing the way they relate, the group (a church, a vestry, a team) is able to achieve something they could not achieve individually.

A servant leader can be calm or boisterous, quiet or animated, outgoing or shy. Remember the example Jesus gave us. He could be intense as he drove

---

95. Robert Greenleaf, "The Servant as Leader," essay (Indianapolis: The Robert K. Greenleaf Center, 1991), 7.

the moneychangers out of the temple or quiet in prayer as he sought his Father in the garden. The outward demeanor does not indicate the shape of a servant leader.

The shape of a servant leader is in her or his motivation. This motivation is grounded in the desire to release the gifts, strengths, talents, and potential among those for whom the leader serves. The alternative is leadership that seeks recognition or pride or control or need for importance. The servant leader is as much concerned with the goal of the project or agenda as he or she is with the process or means used to get to the destination. The group discovers the destination collaboratively and all share the benefit of the journey.

Servant leadership lies at the heart of Christian leadership. While all Christians are called to be servants, it is the special calling of leaders to model Jesus' command to love our neighbors and to follow Jesus' example of washing his friends' feet.

All followers of Jesus who intend to exemplify his style and approach will continually ask these questions:

- How am I leading? Is it with integrity? Is it with the good of all in mind?
- Am I leading effectively? Are we moving toward our destination collegially?
- Are those being served growing as persons? Are they likely to become servants themselves?
- Along the way, do I demonstrate a servant's attitude?
- How am I affecting "the least of these" as I go?
- Am I, as a servant leader, growing?

For further study, please see:

Robert K. Greenleaf, *Servant Leadership: A Journey into the Nature of Legitimate Power and Greatness* (Mahwah, NJ: Paulist Press, 2002).

Robert K. Greenleaf, *The Servant-Leader Within: A Transformativel Path* (Mahwah, NJ: Paulist Press, 2003).

Robert K. Greenleaf, *The Power of Servant Leadership*, ed. Larry C. Spears (San Francisco: Berrett-Koehler Publishers, 1998).